THIRD EDITION

Think Python

How to Think Like a Computer Scientist

Allen B. Downey

Beijing · Boston · Farnham · Sebastopol · Tokyo

Think Python

by Allen B. Downey

Copyright © 2024 Allen B. Downey. All rights reserved.

Published by O'Reilly Media, Inc., 1005 Gravenstein Highway North, Sebastopol, CA 95472.

O'Reilly books may be purchased for educational, business, or sales promotional use. Online editions are also available for most titles (*https://oreilly.com*). For more information, contact our corporate/institutional sales department: 800-998-9938 or *corporate@oreilly.com*.

Acquisitions Editor: Brian Guerin
Development Editor: Jeff Bleiel
Production Editor: Christopher Faucher
Copyeditor: Sonia Saruba
Proofreader: Kim Cofer

Indexer: Ellen Troutman-Zaig
Interior Designer: David Futato
Cover Designer: Karen Montgomery
Illustrator: Kate Dullea

August 2012:   First Edition
December 2015:   Second Edition
June 2024:   Third Edition

Revision History for the Third Edition
2024-05-24:   First Release

See *http://oreilly.com/catalog/errata.csp?isbn=9781098155438* for release details.

The O'Reilly logo is a registered trademark of O'Reilly Media, Inc. *Think Python*, the cover image, and related trade dress are trademarks of O'Reilly Media, Inc.

978-1-098-15543-8

[LSI]

Table of Contents

Preface

Who Is This Book For?

If you want to learn to program, you have come to the right place. Python is one of the best programming languages for beginners—and it is also one of the most in-demand skills.

You have also come at the right time, because learning to program now is probably easier than ever. With virtual assistants like ChatGPT, you don't have to learn alone. Throughout this book, I'll suggest ways you can use these tools to accelerate your learning.

This book is primarily for people who have never programmed before and people who have some experience in another programming language. If you have substantial experience in Python, you might find the first few chapters too slow.

One of the challenges of learning to program is that you have to learn *two* languages: one is the programming language itself; the other is the vocabulary we use to talk about programs. If you learn only the programming language, you are likely to have problems when you need to interpret an error message, read documentation, talk to another person, or use virtual assistants. If you have done some programming, but you have not also learned this second language, I hope you find this book helpful.

Goals of the Book

Writing this book, I tried to be careful with the vocabulary. I define each term when it first appears. And there is a glossary at the end of each chapter that reviews the terms that were introduced.

I also tried to be concise. The less mental effort it takes to read the book, the more capacity you will have for programming.

But you can't learn to program just by reading a book—you have to practice. For that reason, this book includes exercises at the end of every chapter where you can practice what you have learned.

If you read carefully and work on exercises consistently, you will make progress. But I'll warn you now—learning to program is not easy, and even for experienced programmers it can be frustrating. As we go, I will suggest strategies to help you write correct programs and fix incorrect ones.

Navigating the Book

Each chapter in this book builds on the previous ones, so you should read them in order and take time to work on the exercises before you move on.

The first six chapters introduce basic elements like arithmetic, conditionals, and loops. They also introduce the most important concept in programming, functions, and a powerful way to use them, recursion.

Chapters 7 and 8 introduce strings—which can represent letters, words, and sentences—and algorithms for working with them.

Chapters 9 through 12 introduce Python's core data structures—lists, dictionaries, and tuples—which are powerful tools for writing efficient programs. Chapter 12 presents algorithms for analyzing text and randomly generating new text. Algorithms like these are at the core of large language models (LLMs), so this chapter will give you an idea of how tools like ChatGPT work.

Chapter 13 is about ways to store data in long-term storage—files and databases. As an exercise, you can write a program that searches a filesystem and finds duplicate files.

Chapters 14 through 17 introduce object-oriented programming (OOP), which is a way to organize programs and the data they work with. Many Python libraries are written in object-oriented style, so these chapters will help you understand their design—and define your own objects.

The goal of this book is not to cover the entire Python language. Rather, I focus on a subset of the language that provides the greatest capability with the fewest concepts. Nevertheless, Python has a lot of features you can use to solve common problems efficiently. Chapter 18 presents some of these features.

Finally, Chapter 19 presents my parting thoughts and suggestions for continuing your programming journey.

What's New in the Third Edition?

The biggest changes in this edition were driven by two new technologies—Jupyter notebooks and virtual assistants.

Each chapter of this book is a Jupyter notebook, which is a document that contains both ordinary text and code. For me, that makes it easier to write the code, test it, and keep it consistent with the text. For you, it means you can run the code, modify it, and work on the exercises, all in one place. Instructions for working with the notebooks are in the first chapter.

The other big change is that I've added advice for working with virtual assistants like ChatGPT and using them to accelerate your learning. When the previous edition of this book was published in 2015, the predecessors of these tools were far less useful and most people were unaware of them. Now they are a standard tool for software engineering, and I think they will be a transformational tool for learning to program —and learning a lot of other things, too.

The other changes in the book were motivated by my regrets about the second edition. The first is that I did not emphasize software testing. That was already a regrettable omission in 2015, but with the advent of virtual assistants, automated testing has become even more important. So this edition presents Python's most widely used testing tools, `doctest` and `unittest`, and includes several exercises where you can practice working with them.

My other regret is that the exercises in the second edition were uneven—some were more interesting than others and some were too hard. Moving to Jupyter notebooks helped me develop and test a more engaging and effective sequence of exercises.

In this revision, the sequence of topics is almost the same, but I rearranged a few of the chapters and compressed two short chapters into one. Also, I expanded the coverage of strings to include regular expressions.

A few chapters use turtle graphics. In previous editions, I used Python's `turtle` module, but unfortunately it doesn't work in Jupyter notebooks. So I replaced it with a new turtle module that should be easier to use.

Finally, I rewrote a substantial fraction of the text, clarifying places that needed it and cutting back in places where I was not as concise as I could be.

I am very proud of this new edition—I hope you like it!

Getting Started

For most programming languages, including Python, there are many tools you can use to write and run programs. These tools are called integrated development environments (IDEs). In general, there are two kinds of IDEs:

- Some work with files that contain code, so they provide tools for editing and running these files.
- Others work primarily with notebooks, which are documents that contain text and code.

For beginners, I recommend starting with a notebook development environment like Jupyter. The notebooks for this book are available from an online repository at *https://allendowney.github.io/ThinkPython*. There are two ways to use them:

- You can download the notebooks and run them on your own computer. In that case, you have to install Python and Jupyter, which is not hard, but if you want to learn Python, it can be frustrating to spend a lot of time installing software.
- An alternative is to run the notebooks on Colab, which is a Jupyter environment that runs in a web browser, so you don't have to install anything. Colab is operated by Google, and it is free to use.

If you are just getting started, I strongly recommend you start with Colab.

Resources for Teachers

If you are teaching with this book, here are some resources you might find useful.

- You can find notebooks with solutions to the exercises, along with links to the additional resources listed here, at *https://allendowney.github.io/ThinkPython*.
- Quizzes for each chapter, and a summative quiz for the whole book, are available in the O'Reilly Learning Platform version of this book (*https://oreil.ly/think-python-3e*).
- *Teaching and Learning with Jupyter* is an online book with suggestions for using Jupyter effectively in the classroom. You can read the book at *https://jupyter4edu.github.io/jupyter-edu-book*.
- One of the best ways to use notebooks is live coding, where an instructor writes code and students follow along in their own notebooks. To learn about live coding—and get other great advice about teaching programming—I recommend the instructor training provided by The Carpentries, at *https://carpentries.github.io/instructor-training*.

Conventions Used in This Book

The following typographical conventions are used in this book:

Italic
: Indicates new terms, URLs, email addresses, filenames, and file extensions.

Bold
: Indicates the first introduction of new technical term, which also has a corresponding glossary entry.

`Constant width`
: Used for program listings, as well as within paragraphs to refer to program elements such as variable or function names, databases, data types, environment variables, statements, and keywords.

Using Code Examples

Supplemental material (code examples, exercises, etc.) is available for download at *https://allendowney.github.io/ThinkPython*.

If you have a technical question or a problem using the code examples, please send email to *support@oreilly.com*.

This book is here to help you get your job done. In general, if example code is offered with this book, you may use it in your programs and documentation. You do not need to contact us for permission unless you're reproducing a significant portion of the code. For example, writing a program that uses several chunks of code from this book does not require permission. Selling or distributing examples from O'Reilly books does require permission. Answering a question by citing this book and quoting example code does not require permission. Incorporating a significant amount of example code from this book into your product's documentation does require permission.

We appreciate, but generally do not require, attribution. An attribution usually includes the title, author, publisher, and ISBN. For example: "*Think Python* by Allen B. Downey (O'Reilly). Copyright 2024 Allen B. Downey, 978-1-098-15543-8."

If you feel your use of code examples falls outside fair use or the permission given above, feel free to contact us at *permissions@oreilly.com*.

O'Reilly Online Learning

O'REILLY® For more than 40 years, *O'Reilly Media* has provided technology and business training, knowledge, and insight to help companies succeed.

Our unique network of experts and innovators share their knowledge and expertise through books, articles, and our online learning platform. O'Reilly's online learning platform gives you on-demand access to live training courses, in-depth learning paths, interactive coding environments, and a vast collection of text and video from O'Reilly and 200+ other publishers. For more information, visit *https://oreilly.com*.

How to Contact Us

Please address comments and questions concerning this book to the publisher:

O'Reilly Media, Inc.
1005 Gravenstein Highway North
Sebastopol, CA 95472
800-889-8969 (in the United States or Canada)
707-827-7019 (international or local)
707-829-0104 (fax)
support@oreilly.com
https://www.oreilly.com/about/contact.html

We have a web page for this book, where we list errata, examples, and any additional information. You can access this page at *https://oreil.ly/think-python-3e*.

For news and information about our books and courses, visit *https://oreilly.com*.

Find us on LinkedIn: *https://linkedin.com/company/oreilly-media*

Watch us on YouTube: *https://youtube.com/oreillymedia*

Acknowledgments

Many thanks to Jeff Elkner, who translated my Java book into Python, which got this project started and introduced me to what has turned out to be my favorite language. Thanks also to Chris Meyers, who contributed several sections to *How to Think Like a Computer Scientist* (Green Tea Press).

Thanks to the Free Software Foundation for developing the GNU Free Documentation License, which helped make my collaboration with Jeff and Chris possible, and thanks to the Creative Commons for the license I am using now.

Thanks to the developers and maintainers of the Python language and the libraries I used, including the turtle graphics module; the tools I used to develop the book, including Jupyter and JupyterBook; and the services I used, including ChatGPT, Copilot, Colab, and GitHub.

Thanks to the editors at Lulu who worked on *How to Think Like a Computer Scientist* and the editors at O'Reilly Media who worked on *Think Python*.

Special thanks to the technical reviewers for the second edition, Melissa Lewis and Luciano Ramalho, and for the third edition, Sam Lau and Luciano Ramalho (again!). I am also grateful to Luciano for developing the turtle graphics module I use in several chapters, called `jupyturtle`.

Thanks to all the students who worked with earlier versions of this book and all the contributors who sent in corrections and suggestions. More than one hundred sharp-eyed and thoughtful readers have sent in suggestions and corrections over the past few years. Their contributions, and enthusiasm for this project, have been a huge help.

If you have a suggestion or correction, please email *feedback@thinkpython.com*. If you include at least part of the sentence the error appears in, that makes it easy for me to search. Page and section numbers are fine, too, but not quite as easy to work with. Thanks!

CHAPTER 1

Programming as a Way of Thinking

The first goal of this book is to teach you how to program in Python. But learning to program means learning a new way to think, so the second goal of this book is to help you think like a computer scientist. This way of thinking combines some of the best features of mathematics, engineering, and natural science. Like mathematicians, computer scientists use formal languages to denote ideas—specifically computations. Like engineers, they design things, assembling components into systems and evaluating trade-offs among alternatives. Like scientists, they observe the behavior of complex systems, form hypotheses, and test predictions.

We will start with the most basic elements of programming and work our way up. In this chapter, we'll see how Python represents numbers, letters, and words. And you'll learn to perform arithmetic operations.

You will also start to learn the vocabulary of programming, including terms like operator, expression, value, and type. This vocabulary is important—you will need it to understand the rest of the book, to communicate with other programmers, and to use and understand virtual assistants.

Arithmetic Operators

An **arithmetic operator** is a symbol that represents an arithmetic computation. For example, the plus sign, +, performs addition:

```
30 + 12
```

```
42
```

The minus sign, -, is the operator that performs subtraction:

```
43 - 1
```

```
42
```

The asterisk, *, performs multiplication:

```
6 * 7
```

```
42
```

And the forward slash, /, performs division:

```
84 / 2
```

```
42.0
```

Notice that the result of the division is 42.0 rather than 42. That's because there are two types of numbers in Python:

- **integers**, which represent whole numbers, and
- **floating-point numbers**, which represent numbers with a decimal point.

If you add, subtract, or multiply two integers, the result is an integer. But if you divide two integers, the result is a floating-point number. Python provides another operator, //, that performs **integer division**. The result of integer division is always an integer:

```
84 // 2
```

```
42
```

Integer division is also called "floor division" because it always rounds down (toward the "floor"):

```
85 // 2
```

```
42
```

Finally, the operator ** performs exponentiation; that is, it raises a number to a power:

```
7 ** 2
```

49

In some other languages, the caret, ^, is used for exponentiation, but in Python it is a bitwise operator called XOR. If you are not familiar with bitwise operators, the result might be unexpected:

```
7 ^ 2
```

5

I won't cover bitwise operators in this book, but you can read about them at *http:// wiki.python.org/moin/BitwiseOperators*.

Expressions

A collection of operators and numbers is called an **expression**. An expression can contain any number of operators and numbers. For example, here's an expression that contains two operators:

```
6 + 6 ** 2
```

42

Notice that exponentiation happens before addition. Python follows the order of operations you might have learned in a math class: exponentiation happens before multiplication and division, which happen before addition and subtraction.

In the following example, multiplication happens before addition:

```
12 + 5 * 6
```

42

If you want the addition to happen first, you can use parentheses:

```
(12 + 5) * 6
```

102

Every expression has a **value**. For example, the expression 6 * 7 has the value 42.

Arithmetic Functions

In addition to the arithmetic operators, Python provides a few **functions** that work with numbers. For example, the round function takes a floating-point number and rounds it off to the nearest whole number:

```
round(42.4)
```

```
42
```

```
round(42.6)
```

```
43
```

The abs function computes the absolute value of a number. For a positive number, the absolute value is the number itself:

```
abs(42)
```

```
42
```

For a negative number, the absolute value is positive:

```
abs(-42)
```

```
42
```

When we use a function like this, we say we're **calling** the function. An expression that calls a function is a **function call**.

When you call a function, the parentheses are required. If you leave them out, you get an error message:

```
abs 42
```

```
  Cell In[18], line 1
    abs 42
        ^
SyntaxError: invalid syntax
```

You can ignore the first line of this message; it doesn't contain any information we need to understand right now. The second line is the code that contains the error, with a caret (^) beneath it to indicate where the error was discovered.

The last line indicates that this is a **syntax error**, which means that there is something wrong with the structure of the expression. In this example, the problem is that a function call requires parentheses.

Let's see what happens if you leave out the parentheses *and* the value:

```
abs
```

```
<function abs(x, /)>
```

A function name all by itself is a legal expression that has a value. When it's displayed, the value indicates that `abs` is a function, and it includes some additional information I'll explain later.

Strings

In addition to numbers, Python can also represent sequences of letters, which are called **strings** because the letters are strung together like beads on a necklace. To write a string, we can put a sequence of letters inside straight quotation marks:

```
'Hello'
```

```
'Hello'
```

It is also legal to use double quotation marks:

```
"world"
```

```
'world'
```

Double quotes make it easy to write a string that contains an apostrophe, which is the same symbol as a straight quote:

```
"it's a small "
```

```
"it's a small "
```

Strings can also contain spaces, punctuation, and digits:

```
'Well, '
```

```
'Well, '
```

The + operator works with strings; it joins two strings into a single string, which is called **concatenation**:

```
'Well, ' + "it's a small " + 'world.'
```

```
"Well, it's a small world."
```

The * operator also works with strings; it makes multiple copies of a string and concatenates them:

```
'Spam, ' * 4
```

```
'Spam, Spam, Spam, Spam, '
```

The other arithmetic operators don't work with strings.

Python provides a function called len that computes the length of a string:

```
len('Spam')
```

```
4
```

Notice that len counts the letters between the quotes, but not the quotes.

When you create a string, be sure to use straight quotes. The backquote, also known as a backtick, causes a syntax error:

```
`Hello`
```

```
Cell In[49], line 1
    `Hello`
    ^
SyntaxError: invalid syntax
```

Smart quotes, also known as curly quotes, are also illegal.

Values and Types

So far we've seen three kinds of values:

- 2 is an integer,
- 42.0 is a floating-point number, and
- 'Hello' is a string.

A kind of value is called a **type**. Every value has a type—or we sometimes say it "belongs to" a type.

Python provides a function called type that tells you the type of any value. The type of an integer is int:

```
type(2)
```

```
int
```

The type of a floating-point number is float:

```
type(42.0)
```

```
float
```

And the type of a string is str:

```
type('Hello, World!')
```

```
str
```

The types int, float, and str can be used as functions. For example, int can take a floating-point number and convert it to an integer (always rounding down):

```
int(42.9)
```

```
42
```

And float can convert an integer to a floating-point value:

```
float(42)
```

```
42.0
```

Now, here's something that can be confusing. What do you get if you put a sequence of digits in quotes?

```
'126'
```

```
'126'
```

It looks like a number, but it is actually a string:

```
type('126')
```

```
str
```

If you try to use it like a number, you might get an error:

```
'126' / 3
```

```
TypeError: unsupported operand type(s) for /: 'str' and 'int'
```

This example generates a TypeError, which means that the values in the expression, which are called **operands**, have the wrong type. The error message indicates that the / operator does not support the types of these values, which are str and int.

If you have a string that contains digits, you can use int to convert it to an integer:

```
int('126') / 3
```

```
42.0
```

If you have a string that contains digits and a decimal point, you can use float to convert it to a floating-point number:

```
float('12.6')
```

```
12.6
```

When you write a large integer, you might be tempted to use commas between groups of digits, as in 1,000,000. This is a legal expression in Python, but the result is not an integer:

```
1,000,000
```

```
(1, 0, 0)
```

Python interprets 1,000,000 as a comma-separated sequence of integers. We'll learn more about this kind of sequence later.

You can use underscores to make large numbers easier to read:

```
1_000_000
```

```
1000000
```

Formal and Natural Languages

Natural languages are the languages people speak, like English, Spanish, and French. They were not designed by people; they evolved naturally.

Formal languages are languages that are designed by people for specific applications. For example, the notation that mathematicians use is a formal language that is particularly good at denoting relationships among numbers and symbols. Similarly, programming languages are formal languages that have been designed to express computations.

Although formal and natural languages have some features in common there are important differences:

Ambiguity
Natural languages are full of ambiguity, which people deal with by using contextual clues and other information. Formal languages are designed to be nearly or completely unambiguous, which means that any program has exactly one meaning, regardless of context.

Redundancy
In order to make up for ambiguity and reduce misunderstandings, natural languages use redundancy. As a result, they are often verbose. Formal languages are less redundant and more concise.

Literalness
Natural languages are full of idiom and metaphor. Formal languages mean exactly what they say.

Because we all grow up speaking natural languages, it is sometimes hard to adjust to formal languages. Formal languages are more dense than natural languages, so it takes longer to read them. Also, the structure is important, so it is not always best to read from top to bottom, left to right. Finally, the details matter. Small errors in spelling and punctuation, which you can get away with in natural languages, can make a big difference in a formal language.

Debugging

Programmers make mistakes. For whimsical reasons, programming errors are called **bugs** and the process of tracking them down is called **debugging**.

Programming, and especially debugging, sometimes brings out strong emotions. If you are struggling with a difficult bug, you might feel angry, sad, or embarrassed.

Preparing for these reactions might help you deal with them. One approach is to think of the computer as an employee with certain strengths, like speed and precision, and particular weaknesses, like lack of empathy and an inability to grasp the big picture.

Your job is to be a good manager: find ways to take advantage of the strengths and mitigate the weaknesses. And find ways to use your emotions to engage with the problem, without letting your reactions interfere with your ability to work effectively.

Learning to debug can be frustrating, but it is a valuable skill that is useful for many activities beyond programming. At the end of each chapter there is a section, like this one, with my suggestions for debugging. I hope they help!

Glossary

arithmetic operator: A symbol, like + and *, that denotes an arithmetic operation like addition or multiplication.

integer: A type that represents whole numbers.

floating-point: A type that represents numbers with fractional parts.

integer division: An operator, //, that divides two numbers and rounds down to an integer.

expression: A combination of variables, values, and operators.

value: An integer, floating-point number, or string—or one of other kinds of values we will see later.

function: A named sequence of statements that performs some useful operation. Functions may or may not take arguments and may or may not produce a result.

function call: An expression—or part of an expression—that runs a function. It consists of the function name followed by an argument list in parentheses.

syntax error: An error in a program that makes it impossible to parse—and therefore impossible to run.

string: A type that represents sequences of characters.

concatenation: Joining two strings end to end.

type: A category of values. The types we have seen so far are integers (type `int`), floating-point numbers (type `float`), and strings (type `str`).

operand: One of the values on which an operator operates.

natural language: Any of the languages that people speak that evolved naturally.

formal language: Any of the languages that people have designed for specific purposes, such as representing mathematical ideas or computer programs. All programming languages are formal languages.

bug: An error in a program.

debugging: The process of finding and correcting errors.

Exercises

Ask a Virtual Assistant

As you work through this book, there are several ways you can use a virtual assistant or chatbot to help you learn:

- If you want to learn more about a topic in the chapter, or anything is unclear, you can ask for an explanation.
- If you are having a hard time with any of the exercises, you can ask for help.

In each chapter, I'll suggest exercises you can do with a virtual assistant, but I encourage you to try things on your own and see what works for you.

Here are some topics you could ask a virtual assistant about:

- Earlier I mentioned bitwise operators but I didn't explain why the value of 7 ^ 2 is 5. Try asking "What are the bitwise operators in Python?" or "What is the value of 7 XOR 2?"
- I also mentioned the order of operations. For more details, ask "What is the order of operations in Python?"
- The round function, which we used to round a floating-point number to the nearest whole number, can take a second argument. Try asking "What are the arguments of the round function?" or "How do I round pi off to three decimal places?"
- There's one more arithmetic operator I didn't mention; try asking "What is the modulus operator in Python?"

Most virtual assistants know about Python, so they answer questions like this pretty reliably. But remember that these tools make mistakes. If you get code from a chatbot, test it!

Exercise

You might wonder what round does if a number ends in 0.5. The answer is that it sometimes rounds up and sometimes rounds down. Try these examples and see if you can figure out what rule it follows:

```
round(42.5)
```

```
42
```

```
round(43.5)
```

```
44
```

If you are curious, ask a virtual assistant, "If a number ends in 0.5, does Python round up or down?"

Exercise

When you learn about a new feature, you should try it out and make mistakes on purpose. That way, you learn the error messages, and when you see them again, you will know what they mean. It is better to make mistakes now and deliberately than later and accidentally.

1. You can use a minus sign to make a negative number like -2. What happens if you put a plus sign before a number? What about 2++2?

2. What happens if you have two values with no operator between them, like 4 2?

3. If you call a function like round(42.5), what happens if you leave out one or both parentheses?

Exercise

Recall that every expression has a value, every value has a type, and we can use the type function to find the type of any value.

What is the type of the value of the following expressions? Make your best guess for each one, and then use type to find out.

- 765
- 2.718
- '2 pi'
- abs(-7)
- abs(-7.0)
- abs
- int
- type

Exercise

The following questions give you a chance to practice writing arithmetic expressions:

1. How many seconds are there in 42 minutes 42 seconds?
2. How many miles are there in 10 kilometers? Hint: there are 1.61 kilometers in a mile.
3. If you run a 10 kilometer race in 42 minutes 42 seconds, what is your average pace in seconds per mile?
4. What is your average pace in minutes and seconds per mile?
5. What is your average speed in miles per hour?

If you already know about variables, you can use them for this exercise. If you don't, you can do the exercise without them—and then we'll see them in the next chapter.

CHAPTER 2

Variables and Statements

In the previous chapter, we used operators to write expressions that perform arithmetic computations.

In this chapter, you'll learn about variables and statements, the `import` statement, and the `print` function. And I'll introduce more of the vocabulary we use to talk about programs, including "argument" and "module."

Variables

A **variable** is a name that refers to a value. To create a variable, we can write an **assignment statement** like this:

```
n = 17
```

An assignment statement has three parts: the name of the variable on the left, the equals operator, =, and an expression on the right. In this example, the expression is an integer. In the following example, the expression is a floating-point number:

```
pi = 3.141592653589793
```

And in the following example, the expression is a string:

```
message = 'And now for something completely different'
```

When you run an assignment statement, there is no output. Python creates the variable and gives it a value, but the assignment statement has no visible effect. However, after creating a variable, you can use it as an expression. So we can display the value of `message` like this:

```
message
```

```
'And now for something completely different'
```

You can also use a variable as part of an expression with arithmetic operators:

```
n + 25
```

```
42
```

```
2 * pi
```

```
6.283185307179586
```

And you can use a variable when you call a function:

```
round(pi)
```

```
3
```

```
len(message)
```

```
42
```

State Diagrams

A common way to represent variables on paper is to write the name with an arrow pointing to its value:

```
n ———→ 17
pi ———→ 3.141592653589793
message ———→ 'And now for something completely different'
```

This kind of figure is called a **state diagram** because it shows what state each of the variables is in (think of it as the variable's state of mind). We'll use state diagrams throughout the book to represent a model of how Python stores variables and their values.

Variable Names

Variable names can be as long as you like. They can contain both letters and numbers, but they can't begin with a number. It is legal to use uppercase letters, but it is conventional to use only lowercase for variable names.

The only punctuation that can appear in a variable name is the underscore character, _. It is often used in names with multiple words, such as your_name or air speed_of_unladen_swallow.

If you give a variable an illegal name, you get a syntax error. The name million! is illegal because it contains punctuation:

```
million! = 1000000
```

```
  Cell In[15], line 1
    million! = 1000000
           ^
SyntaxError: invalid syntax
```

76trombones is illegal because it starts with a number:

```
76trombones = 'big parade'
```

```
  Cell In[16], line 1
    76trombones = 'big parade'
     ^
SyntaxError: invalid decimal literal
```

class is also illegal, but it might not be obvious why:

```
        class = 'Self-Defence Against Fresh Fruit'
```

```
  Cell In[17], line 1
    class = 'Self-Defence Against Fresh Fruit'
          ^
SyntaxError: invalid syntax
```

It turns out that class is a **keyword**, which is a special word used to specify the structure of a program. Keywords can't be used as variable names.

Here's a complete list of Python's keywords:

```
False     await     else      import    pass
None      break     except    in        raise
True      class     finally   is        return
and       continue  for       lambda    try
as        def       from      nonlocal  while
assert    del       global    not       with
async     elif      if        or        yield
```

You don't have to memorize this list. In most development environments, keywords are displayed in a different color; if you try to use one as a variable name, you'll know.

The import Statement

In order to use some Python features, you have to **import** them. For example, the following statement imports the `math` module:

```
import math
```

A **module** is a collection of variables and functions. The math module provides a variable called `pi` that contains the value of the mathematical constant denoted π. We can display its value like this:

```
math.pi
```

```
3.141592653589793
```

To use a variable in a module, you have to use the **dot operator** (`.`) between the name of the module and the name of the variable.

The math module also contains functions. For example, `sqrt` computes square roots:

```
math.sqrt(25)
```

```
5.0
```

And `pow` raises one number to the power of a second number:

```
math.pow(5, 2)
```

```
25.0
```

At this point we've seen two ways to raise a number to a power: we can use the `math.pow` function or the exponentiation operator, `**`. Either one is fine, but the operator is used more often than the function.

Expressions and Statements

So far, we've seen a few kinds of expressions. An expression can be a single value, like an integer, floating-point number, or string. It can also be a collection of values and operators. And it can include variable names and function calls. Here's an expression that includes several of these elements:

```
19 + n + round(math.pi) * 2
```

```
42
```

We have also seen a few kinds of statements. A **statement** is a unit of code that has an effect, but no value. For example, an assignment statement creates a variable and gives it a value, but the statement itself has no value:

```
n = 17
```

Similarly, an import statement has an effect—it imports a module so we can use the values and functions it contains—but it has no visible effect:

```
import math
```

Computing the value of an expression is called **evaluation**. Running a statement is called **execution**.

The print Function

When you evaluate an expression, the result is displayed:

```
n + 1
```

```
18
```

But if you evaluate more than one expression, only the value of the last one is displayed:

```
n + 2
n + 3
```

```
20
```

To display more than one value, you can use the print function:

```
print(n+2)
print(n+3)
```

```
19
20
```

It also works with floating-point numbers and strings:

```
print('The value of pi is approximately')
print(math.pi)
```

```
The value of pi is approximately
3.141592653589793
```

You can also use a sequence of expressions separated by commas:

```
print('The value of pi is approximately', math.pi)
```

```
The value of pi is approximately 3.141592653589793
```

Notice that the `print` function puts a space between the values.

Arguments

When you call a function, the expression in parentheses is called an **argument**. Normally I would explain why, but in this case the technical meaning of a term has almost nothing to do with the common meaning of the word, so I won't even try.

Some of the functions we've seen so far take only one argument, like `int`:

```
int('101')
```

```
101
```

Some take two, like `math.pow`:

```
math.pow(5, 2)
```

```
25.0
```

Some can take additional arguments that are optional. For example, `int` can take a second argument that specifies the base of the number:

```
int('101', 2)
```

```
5
```

The sequence of digits `101` in base 2 represents the number 5 in base 10.

`round` also takes an optional second argument, which is the number of decimal places to round off to:

```
round(math.pi, 3)
```

```
3.142
```

Some functions can take any number of arguments, like `print`:

```
print('Any', 'number', 'of', 'arguments')
```

```
Any number of arguments
```

If you call a function and provide too many arguments, that's a `TypeError`:

```
float('123.0', 2)
```

```
TypeError: float expected at most 1 argument, got 2
```

If you provide too few arguments, that's also a `TypeError`:

```
math.pow(2)
```

```
TypeError: pow expected 2 arguments, got 1
```

And if you provide an argument with a type the function can't handle, that's a `Type Error`, too:

```
math.sqrt('123')
```

```
TypeError: must be real number, not str
```

This kind of checking can be annoying when you are getting started, but it helps you detect and correct errors.

Comments

As programs get bigger and more complicated, they get more difficult to read. Formal languages are dense, and it is often difficult to look at a piece of code and figure out what it is doing and why.

For this reason, it is a good idea to add notes to your programs to explain in natural language what the program is doing. These notes are called **comments**, and they start with the # symbol:

```
# number of seconds in 42:42
seconds = 42 * 60 + 42
```

In this case, the comment appears on a line by itself. You can also put comments at the end of a line:

```
miles = 10 / 1.61    # 10 kilometers in miles
```

Everything from the # to the end of the line is ignored—it has no effect on the execution of the program. Comments are most useful when they document non-obvious features of the code. It is reasonable to assume that the reader can figure out *what* the code does; it is more useful to explain *why*.

This comment is redundant with the code and useless:

```
v = 8    # assign 8 to v
```

This comment contains useful information that is not in the code:

```
v = 8    # velocity in miles per hour
```

Good variable names can reduce the need for comments, but long names can make complex expressions hard to read, so there is a trade-off.

Debugging

Three kinds of errors can occur in a program: syntax errors, runtime errors, and semantic errors. It is useful to distinguish among them in order to track them down more quickly:

Syntax error
"Syntax" refers to the structure of a program and the rules about that structure. If there is a syntax error anywhere in your program, Python does not run the program. It displays an error message immediately.

Runtime error
If there are no syntax errors in your program, it can start running. But if something goes wrong, Python displays an error message and stops. This type of error is called a runtime error. It is also called an **exception** because it indicates that something exceptional has happened.

Semantic error
The third type of error is "semantic," which means related to meaning. If there is a semantic error in your program, it runs without generating error messages, but it does not do what you intended. Identifying semantic errors can be tricky because it requires you to work backward by looking at the output of the program and trying to figure out what it is doing.

As we've seen, an illegal variable name is a syntax error:

```
million! = 1000000
```

```
  Cell In[43], line 1
    million! = 1000000
           ^
SyntaxError: invalid syntax
```

If you use an operator with a type it doesn't support, that's a runtime error:

```
'126' / 3
```

```
TypeError: unsupported operand type(s) for /: 'str' and 'int'
```

Finally, here's an example of a semantic error. Suppose we want to compute the average of 1 and 3, but we forget about the order of operations and write this:

```
1 + 3 / 2
```

```
2.5
```

When this expression is evaluated, it does not produce an error message, so there is no syntax error or runtime error. But the result is not the average of 1 and 3, so the program is not correct. This is a semantic error because the program runs but it doesn't do what's intended.

Glossary

variable: A name that refers to a value.

assignment statement: A statement that assigns a value to a variable.

state diagram: A graphical representation of a set of variables and the values they refer to.

keyword: A special word used to specify the structure of a program.

import statement: A statement that reads a module file and creates a module object.

module: A file that contains Python code, including function definitions and sometimes other statements.

dot operator: The operator, ., used to access a function in another module by specifying the module name followed by a dot and the function name.

statement: One or more lines of code that represent a command or action.

evaluate: Perform the operations in an expression in order to compute a value.

execute: Run a statement and do what it says.

argument: A value provided to a function when the function is called. Each argument is assigned to the corresponding parameter in the function.

comment: Text included in a program that provides information about the program but has no effect on its execution.

runtime error: An error that causes a program to display an error message and exit.

exception: An error that is detected while the program is running.

semantic error: An error that causes a program to do the wrong thing, but not to display an error message.

Exercises

Ask a Virtual Assistant

Again, I encourage you to use a virtual assistant to learn more about any of the topics in this chapter.

If you are curious about any of keywords I listed, you could ask "Why is class a keyword?" or "Why can't variable names be keywords?"

You might have noticed that int, float, and str are not Python keywords. They are variables that represent types, and they can be used as functions. So it is *legal* to have a variable or function with one of those names, but it is strongly discouraged. Ask an assistant "Why is it bad to use int, float, and string as variable names?"

Also ask, "What are the built-in functions in Python?" If you are curious about any of them, ask for more information.

In this chapter we imported the math module and used some of the variables and functions it provides. Ask an assistant, "What variables and functions are in the math module?" and "Other than math, what modules are considered core Python?"

Exercise

Repeating my advice from the previous chapter, whenever you learn a new feature, you should make errors on purpose to see what goes wrong.

1. We've seen that n = 17 is legal. What about 17 = n?

2. How about x = y = 1?

3. In some languages every statement ends with a semicolon (;). What happens if you put a semicolon at the end of a Python statement?

---

4. What if you put a period at the end of a statement?

5. What happens if you spell the name of a module wrong and try to import `maath`?

Exercise

Practice using the Python interpreter as a calculator:

Part 1. The volume of a sphere with radius r is $\frac{4}{3}\pi r^3$. What is the volume of a sphere with radius 5? Start with a variable named `radius` and then assign the result to a variable named `volume`. Display the result. Add comments to indicate that `radius` is in centimeters and `volume` is in cubic centimeters.

Part 2. A rule of trigonometry says that for any value of x, $(\cos x)^2 + (\sin x)^2 = 1$. Let's see if it's true for a specific value of x like 42.

Create a variable named x with this value. Then use `math.cos` and `math.sin` to compute the sine and cosine of x, and the sum of their squares.

The result should be close to 1. It might not be exactly 1 because floating-point arithmetic is not exact—it is only approximately correct.

Part 3. In addition to `pi`, the other variable defined in the `math` module is `e`, which represents the base of the natural logarithm, written in math notation as e. If you are not familiar with this value, ask a virtual assistant "What is `math.e`?" Now let's compute e^2 three ways:

1. Use `math.e` and the exponentiation operator (`**`).

2. Use `math.pow` to raise `math.e` to the power 2.

3. Use `math.exp`, which takes as an argument a value, x, and computes e^x.

You might notice that the last result is slightly different from the other two. See if you can find out which is correct.

CHAPTER 3

Functions

In the previous chapter we used several functions provided by Python, like `int` and `float`, and a few provided by the `math` module, like `sqrt` and `pow`. In this chapter, you will learn how to create your own functions and run them. And we'll see how one function can call another. As examples, we'll display lyrics from Monty Python songs. These silly examples demonstrate an important feature—the ability to write your own functions is the foundation of programming.

This chapter also introduces a new statement, the `for` loop, which is used to repeat a computation.

Defining New Functions

A **function definition** specifies the name of a new function and the sequence of statements that run when the function is called. Here's an example:

```
def print_lyrics():
    print("I'm a lumberjack, and I'm okay.")
    print("I sleep all night and I work all day.")
```

`def` is a keyword that indicates that this is a function definition. The name of the function is `print_lyrics`. Anything that's a legal variable name is also a legal function name.

The empty parentheses after the name indicate that this function doesn't take any arguments.

The first line of the function definition is called the **header**—the rest is called the **body**. The header has to end with a colon and the body has to be indented. By convention, indentation is always four spaces. The body of this function is two `print` statements; in general, the body of a function can contain any number of statements of any kind.

Defining a function creates a **function object**, which we can display like this:

```
print_lyrics
```

```
<function __main__.print_lyrics()>
```

The output indicates that `print_lyrics` is a function that takes no arguments. `__main__` is the name of the module that contains `print_lyrics`.

Now that we've defined a function, we can call it the same way we call built-in functions:

```
print_lyrics()
```

```
I'm a lumberjack, and I'm okay.
I sleep all night and I work all day.
```

When the function runs, it executes the statements in the body, which display the first two lines of "The Lumberjack Song."

Parameters

Some of the functions we have seen require arguments; for example, when you call `abs` you pass a number as an argument. Some functions take more than one argument; for example, `math.pow` takes two, the base and the exponent.

Here is a definition for a function that takes an argument:

```
def print_twice(string):
    print(string)
    print(string)
```

The variable name in parentheses is a **parameter**. When the function is called, the value of the argument is assigned to the parameter. For example, we can call `print_twice` like this:

```
print_twice('Dennis Moore, ')
```

```
Dennis Moore,
Dennis Moore,
```

Running this function has the same effect as assigning the argument to the parameter and then executing the body of the function, like this:

```
string = 'Dennis Moore, '
print(string)
print(string)
```

```
Dennis Moore,
Dennis Moore,
```

You can also use a variable as an argument:

```
line = 'Dennis Moore, '
print_twice(line)
```

```
Dennis Moore,
Dennis Moore,
```

In this example, the value of line gets assigned to the parameter string.

Calling Functions

Once you have defined a function, you can use it inside another function. To demonstrate, we'll write functions that print the lyrics of "The Spam Song" (*https://www.song facts.com/lyrics/monty-python/the-spam-song*):

Spam, Spam, Spam, Spam,
Spam, Spam, Spam, Spam,
Spam, Spam,
(Lovely Spam, Wonderful Spam!)
Spam, Spam,

We'll start with the following function, which takes two parameters:

```
def repeat(word, n):
    print(word * n)
```

We can use this function to print the first line of the song, like this:

```
spam = 'Spam, '
repeat(spam, 4)
```

```
Spam, Spam, Spam, Spam,
```

To display the first two lines, we can define a new function that uses `repeat`:

```
def first_two_lines():
    repeat(spam, 4)
    repeat(spam, 4)
```

And then call it like this:

```
first_two_lines()
```

```
Spam, Spam, Spam, Spam,
Spam, Spam, Spam, Spam,
```

To display the last three lines, we can define another function, which also uses `repeat`:

```
def last_three_lines():
    repeat(spam, 2)
    print('(Lovely Spam, Wonderful Spam!)')
    repeat(spam, 2)
```

```
last_three_lines()
```

```
Spam, Spam,
(Lovely Spam, Wonderful Spam!)
Spam, Spam,
```

Finally, we can bring it all together with one function that prints the whole verse:

```
def print_verse():
    first_two_lines()
    last_three_lines()
```

```
print_verse()
```

```
Spam, Spam, Spam, Spam,
Spam, Spam, Spam, Spam,
Spam, Spam,
(Lovely Spam, Wonderful Spam!)
Spam, Spam,
```

When we run `print_verse`, it calls `first_two_lines`, which calls `repeat`, which calls `print`. That's a lot of functions.

Of course, we could have done the same thing with fewer functions, but the point of this example is to show how functions can work together.

Repetition

If we want to display more than one verse, we can use a `for` statement. Here's a simple example:

```
for i in range(2):
    print(i)

0
1
```

The first line is a header that ends with a colon. The second line is the body, which has to be indented.

The first line starts with the keyword `for`, a new variable named `i`, and another keyword, `in`. It uses the `range` function to create a sequence of two values, which are `0` and `1`. In Python, when we start counting, we usually start from `0`.

When the `for` statement runs, it assigns the first value from `range` to `i` and then runs the `print` function in the body, which displays `0`.

When it gets to the end of the body, it loops back around to the header, which is why this statement is called a **loop**. The second time through the loop, it assigns the next value from `range` to `i`, and displays it. Then, because that's the last value from `range`, the loop ends.

Here's how we can use a `for` loop to print two verses of the song:

```
for i in range(2):
    print("Verse", i)
    print_verse()
    print()

Verse 0
Spam, Spam, Spam, Spam,
Spam, Spam, Spam, Spam,
Spam, Spam,
(Lovely Spam, Wonderful Spam!)
Spam, Spam,

Verse 1
Spam, Spam, Spam, Spam,
Spam, Spam, Spam, Spam,
Spam, Spam,
(Lovely Spam, Wonderful Spam!)
Spam, Spam,
```

You can put a `for` loop inside a function. For example, `print_n_verses` takes a parameter named n, which has to be an integer, and displays the given number of verses:

```
def print_n_verses(n):
    for i in range(n):
        print_verse()
        print()
```

In this example, we don't use i in the body of the loop, but there has to be a variable name in the header anyway.

Variables and Parameters Are Local

When you create a variable inside a function, it is **local**, which means that it only exists inside the function. For example, the following function takes two arguments, concatenates them, and prints the result twice:

```
def cat_twice(part1, part2):
    cat = part1 + part2
    print_twice(cat)
```

Here's an example that uses it:

```
line1 = 'Always look on the '
line2 = 'bright side of life.'
cat_twice(line1, line2)
```

```
Always look on the bright side of life.
Always look on the bright side of life.
```

When `cat_twice` runs, it creates a local variable named `cat`, which is destroyed when the function ends. If we try to display it, we get a `NameError`:

```
print(cat)
```

```
NameError: name 'cat' is not defined
```

Outside of the function, `cat` is not defined.

Parameters are also local. For example, outside `cat_twice`, there is no such thing as `part1` or `part2`.

Stack Diagrams

To keep track of which variables can be used where, it is sometimes useful to draw a **stack diagram**. Like state diagrams, stack diagrams show the value of each variable, but they also show the function each variable belongs to.

Each function is represented by a **frame**. A frame is a box with the name of a function on the outside and the parameters and local variables of the function on the inside.

Here's the stack diagram for the previous example:

```
 __main__     line1 ──────→ 'Always look on the '

              line2 ──────→ 'bright side of life.'


 cat_twice    part1 ──────→ 'Always look on the '

              part2 ──────→ 'bright side of life.'

                cat ──────→ 'Always look on the bright side of life.'


print_twice    s ──────→ 'Always look on the bright side of life.'


     print     ? ──────→ 'Always look on the bright side of life.'
```

The frames are arranged in a stack that indicates which function called which, and so on. Reading from the bottom, print was called by print_twice, which was called by cat_twice, which was called by __main__—which is a special name for the topmost frame. When you create a variable outside of any function, it belongs to __main__.

In the frame for print, the question mark indicates that we don't know the name of the parameter. If you are curious, ask a virtual assistant, "What are the parameters of the Python print function?"

Tracebacks

When a runtime error occurs in a function, Python displays the name of the function that was running, the name of the function that called it, and so on, up the stack.

To see an example, I'll define a version of `print_twice` that contains an error—it tries to print `cat`, which is a local variable in another function:

```
def print_twice(string):
    print(cat)          # NameError
    print(cat)
```

Now here's what happens when we run `cat_twice`:

```
cat_twice(line1, line2)
```

```
Traceback (most recent call last):

    File <string>:2

    Cell In[21], line 3 in cat_twice
        print_twice(cat)

    Cell In[26], line 2 in print_twice
        print(cat)              # NameError

NameError: name 'cat' is not defined
```

The error message includes a **traceback**, which shows the function that was running when the error occurred, the function that called it, and so on. In this example, it shows that `cat_twice` called `print_twice`, and the error occurred in a `print_twice`.

The order of the functions in the traceback is the same as the order of the frames in the stack diagram. The function that was running is at the bottom.

Why Functions?

It may not be clear yet why it is worth the trouble to divide a program into functions. There are several reasons:

- Creating a new function gives you an opportunity to name a group of statements, which makes your program easier to read and debug.
- Functions can make a program smaller by eliminating repetitive code. Later, if you make a change, you only have to make it in one place.
- Dividing a long program into functions allows you to debug the parts one at a time and then assemble them into a working whole.
- Well-designed functions are often useful for many programs. Once you write and debug one, you can reuse it.

Debugging

Debugging can be frustrating, but it is also challenging, interesting, and sometimes even fun. And it is one of the most important skills you can learn.

In some ways debugging is like detective work. You are given clues and you have to infer the events that led to the results you see.

Debugging is also like experimental science. Once you have an idea about what is going wrong, you modify your program and try again. If your hypothesis was correct, you can predict the result of the modification, and you take a step closer to a working program. If your hypothesis was wrong, you have to come up with a new one.

For some people, programming and debugging are the same thing; that is, programming is the process of gradually debugging a program until it does what you want. The idea is that you should start with a working program and make small modifications, debugging them as you go.

If you find yourself spending a lot of time debugging, that is often a sign that you are writing too much code before you start tests. If you take smaller steps, you might find that you can move faster.

Glossary

function definition: A statement that creates a function.

header: The first line of a function definition.

body: The sequence of statements inside a function definition.

function object: A value created by a function definition. The name of the function is a variable that refers to a function object.

parameter: A name used inside a function to refer to the value passed as an argument.

loop: A statement that runs one or more statements, often repeatedly.

local variable: A variable defined inside a function, which can only be accessed inside the function.

stack diagram: A graphical representation of a stack of functions, their variables, and the values they refer to.

frame: A box in a stack diagram that represents a function call. It contains the local variables and parameters of the function.

traceback: A list of the functions that are executing, printed when an exception occurs.

Exercises

Ask a Virtual Assistant

By convention, the statements in a function or a `for` loop are indented by four spaces. But not everyone agrees with that convention. If you are curious about the history of this great debate, ask a virtual assistant to "tell me about spaces and tabs in Python."

Virtual assistants are pretty good at writing small functions:

1. Ask your favorite VA to "write a function called `repeat` that takes a string and an integer and prints the string the given number of times."

2. If the result uses a `for` loop, you could ask, "Can you do it without a `for` loop?"

3. Pick any other function in this chapter and ask a virtual assistant to write it. The challenge is to describe the function precisely enough to get what you want. Use the vocabulary you have learned so far in this book.

Virtual assistants are also pretty good at debugging functions:

1. Ask a virtual assistant what's wrong with this version of `print_twice`:

   ```
   def print_twice(string):
       print(cat)
       print(cat)
   ```

And if you get stuck on any of the following exercises, consider asking a virtual assistant for help.

Exercise

Write a function named `print_right` that takes a string named `text` as a parameter and prints the string with enough leading spaces that the last letter of the string is in the 40th column of the display.

Hint: use the `len` function, the string concatenation operator (+), and the string repetition operator (*).

Here's an example that shows how it should work:

```
print_right("Monty")
print_right("Python's")
print_right("Flying Circus")
```

```
                          Monty
                       Python's
                  Flying Circus
```

Exercise

Write a function called `triangle` that takes a string and an integer and draws a triangle with the given height, made up of copies of the string. Here's an example of a triangle with five levels using the string `'L'`:

```
triangle('L', 5)
```

```
L
LL
LLL
LLLL
LLLLL
```

Exercise

Write a function called `rectangle` that takes a string and two integers and draws a rectangle with the given width and height, made up of copies of the string. Here's an example of a rectangle with width 5 and height 4, using the string `'H'`:

```
rectangle('H', 5, 4)
```

```
HHHHH
HHHHH
HHHHH
HHHHH
```

Exercise

The song "99 Bottles of Beer" starts with this verse:

> 99 bottles of beer on the wall,
> 99 bottles of beer.
> Take one down, pass it around,
> 98 bottles of beer on the wall.

Then the second verse is the same, except that it starts with 98 bottles and ends with 97. The song continues—for a very long time—until there are 0 bottles of beer.

Write a function called `bottle_verse` that takes a number as a parameter and displays the verse that starts with the given number of bottles.

Hint: consider starting with a function that can print the first, second, or last line of the verse, and then use it to write `bottle_verse`.

Use this function call to display the first verse:

```
bottle_verse(99)
```

```
99 bottles of beer on the wall
99 bottles of beer
Take one down, pass it around
98 bottles of beer on the wall
```

If you want to print the whole song, you can use this `for` loop, which counts down from 99 to 1. You don't have to completely understand this example—we'll learn more about `for` loops and the `range` function later.

```
for n in range(99, 0, -1):
    bottle_verse(n)
    print()
```

CHAPTER 4

Functions and Interfaces

This chapter introduces a module called `jupyturtle`, which allows you to create simple drawings by giving instructions to an imaginary turtle. We will use this module to write functions that draw squares, polygons, and circles—and to demonstrate **interface design**, which is a way of designing functions that work together.

The jupyturtle Module

To use the `jupyturtle` module, we can import it like this:

```
import jupyturtle
```

Now we can use the functions defined in the module, like `make_turtle` and `forward`:

```
jupyturtle.make_turtle()
jupyturtle.forward(100)
```

`make_turtle` creates a **canvas**, which is a space on the screen where we can draw, and a turtle, which is represented by a circular shell and a triangular head. The circle shows the location of the turtle and the triangle indicates the direction it is facing.

`forward` moves the turtle a given distance in the direction it's facing, drawing a line segment along the way. The distance is in arbitrary units—the actual size depends on your computer's screen.

We will use functions defined in the `jupyturtle` module many times, so it would be nice if we did not have to write the name of the module every time. That's possible if we import the module like this:

```
from jupyturtle import make_turtle, forward
```

This version of the import statement imports `make_turtle` and `forward` from the `jupyturtle` module so we can call them like this:

```
make_turtle()
forward(100)
```

`jupyturtle` provides two other functions we'll use, called `left` and `right`. We'll import them like this:

```
from jupyturtle import left, right
```

`left` causes the turtle to turn left. It takes one argument, which is the angle of the turn in degrees. For example, we can make a 90 degree left turn like this:

```
make_turtle()
forward(50)
left(90)
forward(50)
```

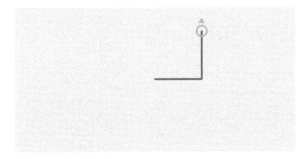

This program moves the turtle east and then north, leaving two line segments behind. Before you go on, see if you can modify the program to make a square.

Making a Square

Here's one way to make a square:

```
make_turtle()

forward(50)
left(90)

forward(50)
left(90)

forward(50)
left(90)

forward(50)
left(90)
```

Because this program repeats the same pair of lines four times, we can do the same thing more concisely with a `for` loop:

```
make_turtle()
for i in range(4):
    forward(50)
    left(90)
```

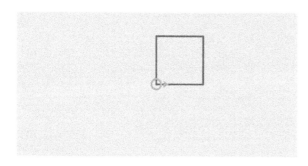

Encapsulation and Generalization

Let's take the square-drawing code from the previous section and put it in a function called square:

```
def square():
    for i in range(4):
        forward(50)
        left(90)
```

Now we can call the function like this:

```
make_turtle()
square()
```

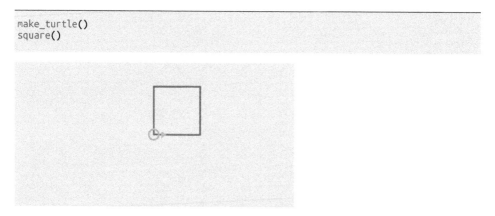

Wrapping a piece of code up in a function is called **encapsulation**. One of the benefits of encapsulation is that it attaches a name to the code, which serves as a kind of documentation. Another advantage is that if you re-use the code, it is more concise to call a function twice than to copy and paste the body!

In the current version, the size of the square is always 50. If we want to draw squares with different sizes, we can take the length of the sides as a parameter:

```
def square(length):
    for i in range(4):
        forward(length)
        left(90)
```

Now we can draw squares with different sizes:

```
make_turtle()
square(30)
square(60)
```

Adding a parameter to a function is called **generalization** because it makes the function more general: with the previous version, the square is always the same size; with this version it can be any size.

If we add another parameter, we can make it even more general. The following function draws regular polygons with a given number of sides:

```
def polygon(n, length):
    angle = 360 / n
    for i in range(n):
        forward(length)
        left(angle)
```

In a regular polygon with n sides, the angle between adjacent sides is 360 / n degrees.

The following example draws a 7-sided polygon with side length of 30:

```
make_turtle()
polygon(7, 30)
```

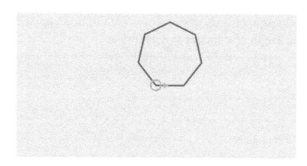

When a function has more than a few numeric arguments, it is easy to forget what they are, or what order they should be in. It can be a good idea to include the names of the parameters in the argument list:

```
make_turtle()
polygon(n=7, length=30)
```

These are sometimes called "named arguments" because they include the parameter names. But in Python they are more often called **keyword arguments** (not to be confused with Python keywords like for and def).

This use of the assignment operator, =, is a reminder about how arguments and parameters work—when you call a function, the arguments are assigned to the parameters.

Approximating a Circle

Now suppose we want to draw a circle. We can do that, approximately, by drawing a polygon with a large number of sides, so each side is small enough that it's hard to see. Here is a function that uses polygon to draw a 30-sided polygon that approximates a circle:

```
import math

def circle(radius):
    circumference = 2 * math.pi * radius
    n = 30
    length = circumference / n
    polygon(n, length)
```

circle takes the radius of the circle as a parameter. It computes circumference, which is the circumference of a circle with the given radius. n is the number of sides, so circumference / n is the length of each side.

This function might take a long time to run. We can speed it up by calling make_turtle with a keyword argument called delay that sets the time, in seconds, the turtle waits after each step. The default value is `0.2` seconds—if we set it to `0.02` it runs about 10 times faster.

```
make_turtle(delay=0.02)
circle(30)
```

A limitation of this solution is that n is a constant, which means that for very big circles, the sides are too long, and for small circles, we waste time drawing very short sides. One option is to generalize the function by taking n as a parameter. But let's keep it simple for now.

Refactoring

Now let's write a more general version of `circle`, called `arc`, that takes a second parameter, `angle`, and draws an arc of a circle that spans the given angle. For example, if `angle` is 360 degrees, it draws a complete circle. If `angle` is 180 degrees, it draws a half circle.

To write `circle`, we were able to reuse `polygon`, because a many-sided polygon is a good approximation of a circle. But we can't use `polygon` to write `arc`.

Instead, we'll create the more general version of `polygon`, called `polyline`:

```
def polyline(n, length, angle):
    for i in range(n):
        forward(length)
        left(angle)
```

`polyline` takes as parameters the number of line segments to draw, n; the length of the segments, `length`; and the angle between them, `angle`.

Now we can rewrite `polygon` to use `polyline`:

```
def polygon(n, length):
    angle = 360.0 / n
    polyline(n, length, angle)
```

And we can use `polyline` to write `arc`:

```
def arc(radius, angle):
    arc_length = 2 * math.pi * radius * angle / 360
    n = 30
    length = arc_length / n
    step_angle = angle / n
    polyline(n, length, step_angle)
```

`arc` is similar to `circle`, except that it computes `arc_length`, which is a fraction of the circumference of a circle.

Finally, we can rewrite `circle` to use `arc`:

```
def circle(radius):
    arc(radius,  360)
```

To check that these functions work as expected, we'll use them to draw something like a snail. With `delay=0`, the turtle runs as fast as possible.

```
make_turtle(delay=0)
polygon(n=20, length=9)
arc(radius=70, angle=70)
circle(radius=10)
```

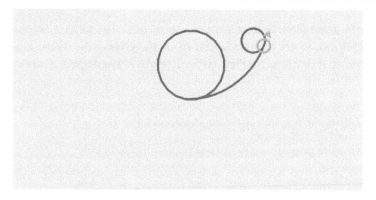

In this example, we started with working code and reorganized it with different functions. Changes like this, which improve the code without changing its behavior, are called **refactoring**.

If we had planned ahead, we might have written `polyline` first and avoided refactoring, but often you don't know enough at the beginning of a project to design all the functions. Once you start coding, you understand the problem better. Sometimes refactoring is a sign that you have learned something.

Stack Diagram

When we call `circle`, it calls `arc`, which calls `polyline`. We can use a stack diagram to show this sequence of function calls and the parameters for each one:

circle   radius ──→ 30

    arc   radius ──→ 30   angle ──→ 360

polyline   n ──→ 60   length ──→ 3.04   angle ──→ 5.8

Notice that the value of `angle` in `polyline` is different from the value of `angle` in `arc`. Parameters are local, which means you can use the same parameter name in different functions; it's a different variable in each function, and it can refer to a different value.

A Development Plan

A **development plan** is a process for writing programs. The process we used in this chapter is "encapsulation and generalization." The steps of this process are:

1. Start by writing a small program with no function definitions.
2. Once you get the program working, identify a coherent piece of it, encapsulate the piece in a function, and give it a name. Copy and paste working code to avoid retyping (and re-debugging).
3. Generalize the function by adding appropriate parameters.
4. Repeat steps 1 through 3 until you have a set of working functions.
5. Look for opportunities to improve the program by refactoring. For example, if you have similar code in several places, consider factoring it into an appropriately general function.

This process has some drawbacks—we will see alternatives later—but it can be useful if you don't know ahead of time how to divide the program into functions. This approach lets you design as you go along.

The design of a function has two parts:

interface
How the function is used, including its name, the parameters it takes, and what the function is supposed to do

implementation
How the function does what it's supposed to do

For example, here's the first version of `circle` we wrote, which uses `polygon`:

```
def circle(radius):
    circumference = 2 * math.pi * radius
    n = 30
    length = circumference / n
    polygon(n, length)
```

And here's the refactored version that uses `arc`:

```
def circle(radius):
    arc(radius,  360)
```

These two functions have the same interface—they take the same parameters and do the same thing—but they have different implementations.

Docstrings

A **docstring** is a string at the beginning of a function that explains the interface ("doc" is short for "documentation"). Here is an example:

```
def polyline(n, length, angle):
    """Draws line segments with the given length and angle between them.

    n: integer number of line segments
    length: length of the line segments
    angle: angle between segments (in degrees)
    """
    for i in range(n):
        forward(length)
        left(angle)
```

By convention, docstrings are triple-quoted strings, also known as **multiline strings** because the triple quotes allow the string to span more than one line.

A docstring should:

- Explain concisely what the function does, without getting into the details of how it works,
- Explain what effect each parameter has on the behavior of the function, and
- Indicate what type each parameter should be, if it is not obvious.

Writing this kind of documentation is an important part of interface design. A well-designed interface should be simple to explain; if you have a hard time explaining one of your functions, maybe the interface could be improved.

Debugging

An interface is like a contract between a function and a caller. The caller agrees to provide certain arguments and the function agrees to do certain work.

For example, `polyline` requires three arguments: `n` has to be an integer, `length` should be a positive number, and `angle` has to be a number, which is understood to be in degrees.

These requirements are called **preconditions** because they are supposed to be true before the function starts executing. Conversely, conditions at the end of the function are **postconditions**. Postconditions include the intended effect of the function (like drawing line segments) and any side effects (like moving the turtle or making other changes).

Preconditions are the responsibility of the caller. If the caller violates a precondition and the function doesn't work correctly, the bug is in the caller, not the function.

If the preconditions are satisfied and the postconditions are not, the bug is in the function. If your pre- and postconditions are clear, they can help with debugging.

Glossary

interface design: A process for designing the interface of a function, which includes the parameters it should take.

canvas: A window used to display graphical elements including lines, circles, rectangles, and other shapes.

encapsulation: The process of transforming a sequence of statements into a function definition.

generalization: The process of replacing something unnecessarily specific (like a number) with something appropriately general (like a variable or parameter).

keyword argument: An argument that includes the name of the parameter.

refactoring: The process of modifying a working program to improve function interfaces and other qualities of the code.

development plan: A process for writing programs.

docstring: A string that appears at the top of a function definition to document the function's interface.

multiline string: A string enclosed in triple quotes that can span more than one line of a program.

precondition: A requirement that should be satisfied by the caller before a function starts.

postcondition: A requirement that should be satisfied by the function before it ends.

Exercises

For these exercises, there are a few more turtle functions you might want to use:

penup
> Lift the turtle's imaginary pen so it doesn't leave a trail when it moves.

pendown
> Put the pen back down.

The following function uses penup and pendown to move the turtle without leaving a trail:

```
from jupyturtle import penup, pendown

def jump(length):
    """Move forward length units without leaving a trail.

    Postcondition: Leaves the pen down.
    """
    penup()
    forward(length)
    pendown()
```

Exercise

Write a function called rectangle that draws a rectangle with given side lengths. For example, here's a rectangle that's 80 units wide and 40 units tall:

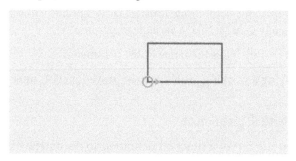

Exercise

Write a function called rhombus that draws a rhombus with a given side length and a given interior angle. For example, here's a rhombus with side length of 50 and an interior angle of 60 degrees:

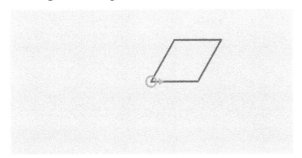

Exercise

Now write a more general function called parallelogram that draws a quadrilateral with parallel sides. Then rewrite rectangle and rhombus to use parallelogram.

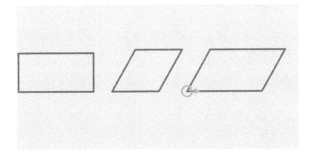

Exercise

Write an appropriately general set of functions that can draw shapes like this.

Hint: write a function called `triangle` that draws one triangular segment, and then a function called `draw_pie` that uses `triangle`.

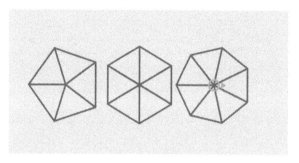

Exercise

Write an appropriately general set of functions that can draw flowers like this.

Hint: use `arc` to write a function called `petal` that draws one flower petal.

Ask a Virtual Assistant

Several modules like `jupyturtle` in Python, and the one we used in this chapter have been customized for this book. So if you ask a virtual assistant for help, it won't know which module to use. But if you give it a few examples to work with, it can probably figure it out. For example, try this prompt and see if it can write a function that draws a spiral:

```
The following program uses a turtle graphics module to draw a circle:

from jupyturtle import make_turtle, forward, left
import math

def polygon(n, length):
    angle = 360 / n
    for i in range(n):
        forward(length)
        left(angle)

def circle(radius):
    circumference = 2 * math.pi * radius
    n = 30
    length = circumference / n
    polygon(n, length)

make_turtle(delay=0)
circle(30)

Write a function that draws a spiral.
```

Keep in mind that the result might use features we have not seen yet, and it might have errors. Copy the code from the virtual assistant and see if you can get it working. If you didn't get what you wanted, try modifying the prompt.

CHAPTER 5

Conditionals and Recursion

The main topic of this chapter is the if statement, which executes different code depending on the state of the program. With the if statement we'll be able to explore one of the most powerful ideas in computing, **recursion**.

But we'll start with three new features: the modulus operator, boolean expressions, and logical operators.

Integer Division and Modulus

Recall that the integer division operator, //, divides two numbers and rounds down to an integer. For example, suppose the runtime of a movie is 105 minutes. You might want to know how long that is in hours. Conventional division returns a floating-point number:

```
minutes = 105
minutes / 60
```

```
1.75
```

But we don't normally write hours with decimal points. Floor division returns the integer number of hours, rounding down:

```
minutes = 105
hours = minutes // 60
hours
```

```
1
```

To get the remainder, you could subtract off one hour, in minutes:

```
remainder = minutes - hours * 60
remainder
```

45

Or you could use the **modulus operator**, %, which divides two numbers and returns the remainder:

```
remainder = minutes % 60
remainder
```

45

The modulus operator is more useful than it might seem. For example, it can check whether one number is divisible by another: if x % y is zero, then x is divisible by y.

Also, it can extract the rightmost digit or digits from a number. For example, x % 10 yields the rightmost digit of x (in base 10). Similarly, x % 100 yields the last two digits.

Finally, the modulus operator can do "clock arithmetic." For example, if an event starts at 11 A.M. and lasts three hours, we can use the modulus operator to figure out what time it ends:

```
start = 11
duration = 3
end = (start + duration) % 12
end
```

2

The event would end at 2 P.M.:

```
a = 25 // 10
b = 25 % 10
a, b
```

(2, 5)

Boolean Expressions

A **boolean expression** is an expression that is either true or false. For example, the following expressions use the equals operator, ==, which compares two values and produces True if they are equal and False otherwise:

```
5 == 5
```

True

```
5 == 7
```

False

A common error is to use a single equals sign (=) instead of a double equals sign (==). Remember that = assigns a value to a variable and == compares two values:

```
x = 5
y = 7
```

```
x == y
```

False

True and False are special values that belong to the type bool; they are not strings:

```
type(True)
```

bool

```
type(False)
```

bool

The == operator is one of the **relational operators**; the others are:

```
x != y          # x is not equal to y
```

True

```
x > y           # x is greater than y
```

False

```
x < y           # x is less than to y
```

True

```
x >= y              # x is greater than or equal to y
```

```
False
```

```
x <= y              # x is less than or equal to y
```

```
True
```

Logical Operators

To combine boolean values into expressions, we can use **logical operators**. The most common are and, or, and not. The meaning of these operators is similar to their meaning in English. For example, the value of the following expression is True only if x is greater than 0 *and* less than 10:

```
x > 0 and x < 10
```

```
True
```

The following expression is True if *either or both* of the conditions is true, that is, if the number is divisible by 2 *or* 3:

```
x % 2 == 0 or x % 3 == 0
```

```
False
```

Finally, the not operator negates a boolean expression, so the following expression is True if x > y is False:

```
not x > y
```

```
True
```

Strictly speaking, the operands of a logical operator should be boolean expressions, but Python is not very strict. Any nonzero number is interpreted as True:

```
42 and True
```

```
True
```

This flexibility can be useful, but there are some subtleties to it that can be confusing. You might want to avoid it.

if Statements

In order to write useful programs, we almost always need the ability to check conditions and change the behavior of the program accordingly. **Conditional statements** give us this ability. The simplest form is the if statement:

```
if x > 0:
    print('x is positive')
```

```
x is positive
```

if is a Python keyword. if statements have the same structure as function definitions: a header followed by an indented statement or sequence of statements called a **block**.

The boolean expression after if is called the **condition**. If it is true, the statements in the indented block run. If not, they don't.

There is no limit to the number of statements that can appear in the block, but there has to be at least one. Occasionally, it is useful to have a block that does nothing—usually as a place keeper for code you haven't written yet. In that case, you can use the pass statement, which does nothing:

```
if x < 0:
    pass          # TODO: need to handle negative values!
```

The word TODO in a comment is a conventional reminder that there's something you need to do later.

The else Clause

An if statement can have a second part, called an else clause. The syntax looks like this:

```
if x % 2 == 0:
    print('x is even')
else:
    print('x is odd')
```

```
x is odd
```

If the condition is true, the first indented statement runs; otherwise, the second indented statement runs.

In this example, if x is even, the remainder when x is divided by 2 is 0, so the condition is true and the program displays x is even. If x is odd, the remainder is 1, so the condition is false, and the program displays x is odd.

Since the condition must be true or false, exactly one of the alternatives will run. The alternatives are called **branches**.

Chained Conditionals

Sometimes there are more than two possibilities and we need more than two branches. One way to express a computation like that is a **chained conditional**, which includes an elif clause:

```
if x < y:
    print('x is less than y')
elif x > y:
    print('x is greater than y')
else:
    print('x and y are equal')
```

```
x is less than y
```

elif is an abbreviation of "else if." There is no limit on the number of elif clauses. If there is an else clause, it has to be at the end, but there doesn't have to be one.

Each condition is checked in order. If the first is false, the next is checked, and so on. If one of them is true, the corresponding branch runs and the if statement ends. Even if more than one condition is true, only the first true branch runs.

Nested Conditionals

One conditional can also be nested within another. We could have written the example in the previous section like this:

```
if x == y:
    print('x and y are equal')
else:
    if x < y:
        print('x is less than y')
    else:
        print('x is greater than y')
```

```
x is less than y
```

The outer if statement contains two branches. The first branch contains a simple statement. The second branch contains another if statement, which has two branches of its own. Those two branches are both simple statements, although they could have been conditional statements as well.

Although the indentation of the statements makes the structure apparent, **nested conditionals** can be difficult to read. I suggest you avoid them when you can.

Logical operators often provide a way to simplify nested conditional statements. Here's an example with a nested conditional:

```
if 0 < x:
    if x < 10:
        print('x is a positive single-digit number.')
```

```
x is a positive single-digit number.
```

The print statement runs only if we make it past both conditionals, so we get the same effect with the and operator:

```
if 0 < x and x < 10:
    print('x is a positive single-digit number.')
```

```
x is a positive single-digit number.
```

For this kind of condition, Python provides a more concise option:

```
if 0 < x < 10:
    print('x is a positive single-digit number.')
```

```
x is a positive single-digit number.
```

Recursion

It is legal for a function to call itself. It may not be obvious why that is a good thing, but it turns out to be one of the most magical things a program can do. Here's an example:

```
def countdown(n):
    if n <= 0:
        print('Blastoff!')
    else:
        print(n)
        countdown(n-1)
```

If n is 0 or negative, countdown outputs the word, "Blastoff!". Otherwise, it outputs n and then calls itself, passing n-1 as an argument.

Here's what happens when we call this function with the argument 3:

```
countdown(3)
```

```
3
2
1
Blastoff!
```

> The execution of countdown begins with n=3, and since n is greater than 0, it displays 3, and then calls itself...
>
> > The execution of countdown begins with n=2, and since n is greater than 0, it displays 2, and then calls itself...
> >
> > > The execution of countdown begins with n=1, and since n is greater than 0, it displays 1, and then calls itself...
> > >
> > > > The execution of countdown begins with n=0, and since n is not greater than 0, it displays "Blastoff!" and returns.
> > >
> > > The countdown that got n=1 returns.
> >
> > The countdown that got n=2 returns.
>
> The countdown that got n=3 returns.

A function that calls itself is **recursive**. As another example, we can write a function that prints a string n times:

```python
def print_n_times(string, n):
    if n > 0:
        print(string)
        print_n_times(string, n-1)
```

If n is positive, print_n_times displays the value of string and then calls itself, passing along string and n-1 as arguments.

If n is 0 or negative, the condition is false and print_n_times does nothing.

Here's how it works:

```
print_n_times('Spam ', 4)
```

```
Spam
Spam
Spam
Spam
```

For simple examples like this, it is probably easier to use a for loop. But we will see examples later that are hard to write with a for loop and easy to write with recursion, so it is good to start early.

Stack Diagrams for Recursive Functions

Here's a stack diagram that shows the frames created when we called countdown with n = 3:

countdown   n ——→ 3

countdown   n ——→ 2

countdown   n ——→ 1

countdown   n ——→ 0

The four countdown frames have different values for the parameter n. The bottom of the stack, where n=0, is called the **base case**. It does not make a recursive call, so there are no more frames.

Infinite Recursion

If a recursion never reaches a base case, it goes on making recursive calls forever, and the program never terminates. This is known as **infinite recursion**, and it is generally not a good idea. Here's a minimal function with an infinite recursion:

```
def recurse():
    recurse()
```

Every time recurse is called, it calls itself, which creates another frame. In Python, there is a limit to the number of frames that can be on the stack at the same time.

If a program exceeds the limit, it causes a runtime error:

```
recurse()
```

```
 - - - - - - - - - - - - - - - - - - - - - - - - - - - - - - - - - - - - - - - - - - - - - - - - - - -
RecursionError                          Traceback (most recent call last)
Cell In[41], line 1
----> 1 recurse()

Cell In[39], line 2, in recurse()
      1 def recurse():
----> 2     recurse()

Cell In[39], line 2, in recurse()
      1 def recurse():
----> 2     recurse()

    [... skipping similar frames: recurse at line 2 (2958 times)]

Cell In[39], line 2, in recurse()
      1 def recurse():
----> 2     recurse()

RecursionError: maximum recursion depth exceeded
```

The traceback indicates that there were almost three thousand frames on the stack when the error occurred.

If you encounter an infinite recursion by accident, review your function to confirm that there is a base case that does not make a recursive call. And if there is a base case, check whether you are guaranteed to reach it.

Keyboard Input

The programs we have written so far accept no input from the user. They just do the same thing every time.

Python provides a built-in function called input that stops the program and waits for the user to type something. When the user presses Return or Enter the program resumes, and input returns what the user typed as a string:

```
text = input()
```

Before getting input from the user, you might want to display a prompt telling the user what to type. input can take a prompt as an argument:

```
name = input('What...is your name?\n')
name
```

```
What...is your name?
It is Arthur, King of the Britons
```

```
'It is Arthur, King of the Britons'
```

The sequence \n at the end of the prompt represents a **newline**, which is a special character that causes a line break—that way the user's input appears below the prompt.

If you expect the user to type an integer, you can use the int function to convert the return value to int:

```
prompt = 'What...is the airspeed velocity of an unladen swallow?\n'
speed = input(prompt)
speed
```

```
What...is the airspeed velocity of an unladen swallow?
What do you mean: an African or European swallow?
```

```
'What do you mean: an African or European swallow?'
```

But if they type something that's not an integer, you'll get a runtime error.

```
int(speed)
```

```
ValueError: invalid literal for int() with base 10: 'What do you mean:
            an African or European swallow?'
```

We will see how to handle this kind of error later.

Debugging

When a syntax or runtime error occurs, the error message contains a lot of information, but it can be overwhelming. The most useful parts are usually:

- What kind of error it was, and
- Where it occurred.

Syntax errors are usually easy to find, but there are a few gotchas. Errors related to spaces and tabs can be tricky because they are invisible and we are used to ignoring them:

```
x = 5
 y = 6
```

```
Cell In[50], line 2
    y = 6
    ^
IndentationError: unexpected indent
```

In this example, the problem is that the second line is indented by one space. But the error message points to y, which is misleading. Error messages indicate where the problem was discovered, but the actual error might be earlier in the code.

The same is true of runtime errors. For example, suppose you are trying to convert a ratio to decibels, like this:

```
import math
numerator = 9
denominator = 10
ratio = numerator // denominator
decibels = 10 * math.log10(ratio)
```

```
---------------------------------------------------------------
ValueError                          Traceback (most recent call last)
Cell In[52], line 5
      3 denominator = 10
      4 ratio = numerator // denominator
----> 5 decibels = 10 * math.log10(ratio)

ValueError: math domain error
```

The error message indicates line 5, but there is nothing wrong with that line. The problem is in line 4, which uses floor division instead of floating-point division—as a result, the value of ratio is 0. When we call math.log10, we get a ValueError with the message math domain error, because 0 is not in the "domain" of valid arguments for math.log10, because the logarithm of 0 is undefined.

In general, you should take the time to read error messages carefully, but don't assume that everything they say is correct.

Glossary

recursion: The process of calling the function that is currently executing.

modulus operator: An operator, %, that works on integers and returns the remainder when one number is divided by another.

boolean expression: An expression whose value is either `True` or `False`.

relational operator: One of the operators that compares its operands: ==, !=, >, <, >=, and <=.

logical operator: One of the operators that combines boolean expressions, including `and`, `or`, and `not`.

conditional statement: A statement that controls the flow of execution, depending on some condition.

block: One or more statements indented to indicate they are part of another statement.

condition: The boolean expression in a conditional statement that determines which branch runs.

branch: One of the alternative sequences of statements in a conditional statement.

chained conditional: A conditional statement with a series of alternative branches.

nested conditional: A conditional statement that appears in one of the branches of another conditional statement.

recursive: A function that calls itself.

base case: A conditional branch in a recursive function that does not make a recursive call.

infinite recursion: A recursion that doesn't have a base case, or never reaches it. Eventually, an infinite recursion causes a runtime error.

newline: A character that creates a line break between two parts of a string.

Exercises

Ask a Virtual Assistant

- Ask a virtual assistant, "What are some uses of the modulus operator?"
- Python provides operators to compute the logical operations `and`, `or`, and `not`, but it doesn't have an operator that computes the exclusive or operation, usually written `xor`. Ask an assistant "What is the logical `xor` operation and how do I compute it in Python?"

In this chapter, we saw two ways to write an `if` statement with three branches, using a chained conditional or a nested conditional. You can use a virtual assistant to convert from one to the other. For example, ask a virtual assistant, "Convert this statement to a chained conditional":

```
if x == y:
    print('x and y are equal')
else:
    if x < y:
        print('x is less than y')
    else:
        print('x is greater than y')
```

```
x is less than y
```

Ask a virtual assistant, "Rewrite this statement with a single conditional":

```
if 0 < x:
    if x < 10:
        print('x is a positive single-digit number.')
```

```
x is a positive single-digit number.
```

See if a virtual assistant can simplify this unnecessary complexity:

```
if not x <= 0 and not x >= 10:
    print('x is a positive single-digit number.')
```

```
x is a positive single-digit number.
```

Here's an attempt at a recursive function that counts down by two:

```
def countdown_by_two(n):
    if n == 0:
        print('Blastoff!')
    else:
        print(n)
        countdown_by_two(n-2)
```

It seems to work:

```
countdown_by_two(6)
```

```
6
4
2
Blastoff!
```

But it has an error. Ask a virtual assistant what's wrong and how to fix it. Paste the solution it provides here and test it.

Exercise

The `time` module provides a function, also called `time`, that returns the number of seconds since the "Unix epoch," which is January 1, 1970, 00:00:00 UTC (Coordinated Universal Time):

```
from time import time

now = time()
now
```

```
1709908595.7334914
```

Use floor division and the modulus operator to compute the number of days since January 1, 1970, and the current time of day in hours, minutes, and seconds.

Exercise

If you are given three sticks, you may or may not be able to arrange them in a triangle. For example, if one of the sticks is 12 inches long and the other two are 1 inch long, you will not be able to get the short sticks to meet in the middle. For any three lengths, there is a test to see if it is possible to form a triangle:

> If any of the three lengths is greater than the sum of the other two, then you cannot form a triangle. Otherwise, you can. (If the sum of two lengths equals the third, they form what is called a "degenerate" triangle.)

Write a function named `is_triangle` that takes three integers as arguments, and that prints either "Yes" or "No," depending on whether you can or cannot form a triangle from sticks with the given lengths. Hint: use a chained conditional.

Exercise

What is the output of the following program? Draw a stack diagram that shows the state of the program when it prints the result.

```
def recurse(n, s):
    if n == 0:
        print(s)
    else:
        recurse(n-1, n+s)

recurse(3, 0)
```

6

Exercise

The following exercises use the `jupyturtle` module, described in Chapter 4.

Read the following function and see if you can figure out what it does. Then run it and see if you got it right. Adjust the values of `length`, `angle`, and `factor` and see what effect they have on the result. If you are not sure you understand how it works, try asking a virtual assistant.

```
from jupyturtle import forward, left, right, back

def draw(length):
    angle = 50
    factor = 0.6

    if length > 5:
        forward(length)
        left(angle)
        draw(factor * length)
        right(2 * angle)
        draw(factor * length)
        left(angle)
        back(length)
```

Exercise

Ask a virtual assistant, "What is the Koch curve?"

To draw a Koch curve with length x, all you have to do is:

1. Draw a Koch curve with length x/3.

2. Turn left 60 degrees.

3. Draw a Koch curve with length x/3.

4. Turn right 120 degrees.

5. Draw a Koch curve with length x/3.

6. Turn left 60 degrees.

7. Draw a Koch curve with length x/3.

The exception is if x is less than 5—in that case, you can just draw a straight line with length x.

Write a function called koch that takes x as a parameter and draws a Koch curve with the given length. The result should look like this:

```
make_turtle(delay=0)
koch(120)
```

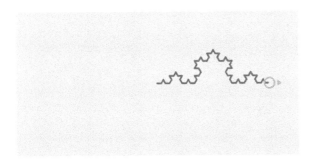

Exercise

Virtual assistants know about the functions in the `jupyturtle` module, but because there are many versions of these functions, with different names, it might not know which one you are talking about.

To solve this problem, you can provide additional information before you ask a question. For example, you could start a prompt with "Here's a program that uses the `jupy turtle` module," and then paste in one of the examples from this chapter. After that, the virtual assistant should be able to generate code that uses this module.

As an example, ask a virtual assistant for a program that draws a Sierpiński triangle. The code you get should be a good starting place, but you might have to do some debugging. If the first attempt doesn't work, you can tell the virtual assistant what happened and ask for help—or you can debug it yourself.

Here's what the result might look like, although the version you get might be different:

```
make_turtle(delay=0, height=200)

draw_sierpinski(100, 3)
```

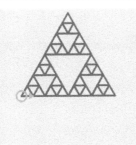

CHAPTER 6

Return Values

In previous chapters, we've used built-in functions—like `abs` and `round`—and functions in the `math` module—like `sqrt` and `pow`. When you call one of these functions, it returns a value you can assign to a variable or use as part of an expression.

The functions we have written so far are different. Some use the `print` function to display values, and some use `Turtle` functions to draw figures. But they don't return values we assign to variables or use in expressions.

In this chapter, we'll see how to write functions that return values.

Some Functions Have Return Values

When you call a function like `math.sqrt`, the result is called a **return value**. If the function call appears at the end of a cell, Jupyter displays the return value immediately:

```
import math

math.sqrt(42 / math.pi)
```

```
3.656366395715726
```

If you assign the return value to a variable, it doesn't get displayed:

```
radius = math.sqrt(42 / math.pi)
```

But you can display it later:

```
radius
```

```
3.656366395715726
```

Or you can use the return value as part of an expression:

```
radius + math.sqrt(42 / math.pi)
```

```
7.312732791431452
```

Here's an example of a function that returns a value:

```
def circle_area(radius):
    area = math.pi * radius**2
    return area
```

circle_area takes radius as a parameter and computes the area of a circle with that radius.

The last line is a return statement that returns the value of area.

If we call the function like this, Jupyter displays the return value:

```
circle_area(radius)
```

```
42.00000000000001
```

We can assign the return value to a variable:

```
a = circle_area(radius)
```

Or use it as part of an expression:

```
circle_area(radius) + 2 * circle_area(radius / 2)
```

```
63.000000000000014
```

Later, we can display the value of the variable we assigned the result to:

```
a
```

```
42.00000000000001
```

But we can't access `area`:

```
area
```

```
NameError: name 'area' is not defined
```

`area` is a local variable in a function, so we can't access it from outside the function.

And Some Have None

If a function doesn't have a `return` statement, it returns None, which is a special value like `True` and `False`. For example, here's the `repeat` function from Chapter 3:

```
def repeat(word, n):
    print(word * n)
```

If we call it like this, it displays the first line of the Monty Python song "Finland":

```
repeat('Finland, ', 3)
```

```
Finland, Finland, Finland,
```

This function uses the `print` function to display a string, but it does not use a `return` statement to return a value. If we assign the result to a variable, it displays the string anyway:

```
result = repeat('Finland, ', 3)
```

```
Finland, Finland, Finland,
```

And if we display the value of the variable, we get nothing:

```
result
```

`result` actually has a value, but Jupyter doesn't show it. However, we can display it like this:

```
print(result)
```

```
None
```

The return value from `repeat` is None.

Now here's a function similar to `repeat` except that it has a return value:

```
def repeat_string(word, n):
    return word * n
```

Notice that we can use an expression in a `return` statement, not just a variable.

With this version, we can assign the result to a variable. When the function runs, it doesn't display anything:

```
line = repeat_string('Spam, ', 4)
```

But later we can display the value assigned to `line`:

```
line
```

```
'Spam, Spam, Spam, Spam, '
```

A function like this is called a **pure function** because it doesn't display anything or have any other effect—other than returning a value.

Return Values and Conditionals

If Python did not provide `abs`, we could write it like this:

```
def absolute_value(x):
    if x < 0:
        return -x
    else:
        return x
```

If x is negative, the first `return` statement returns -x and the function ends immediately. Otherwise, the second `return` statement returns x and the function ends. So this function is correct.

However, if you put `return` statements in a conditional, you have to make sure that every possible path through the program hits a `return` statement. For example, here's an incorrect version of `absolute_value`:

```
def absolute_value_wrong(x):
    if x < 0:
        return -x
    if x > 0:
        return x
```

Here's what happens if we call this function with 0 as an argument:

```
absolute_value_wrong(0)
```

We get nothing! Here's the problem: when x is 0, neither condition is true, and the function ends without hitting a return statement, which means that the return value is None, so Jupyter displays nothing.

As another example, here's a version of absolute_value with an extra return statement at the end:

```
def absolute_value_extra_return(x):
    if x < 0:
        return -x
    else:
        return x

    return 'This is dead code'
```

If x is negative, the first return statement runs and the function ends. Otherwise the second return statement runs and the function ends. Either way, we never get to the third return statement—so it can never run.

Code that can never run is called **dead code**. In general, dead code doesn't do any harm, but it often indicates a misunderstanding, and it might be confusing to someone trying to understand the program.

Incremental Development

As you write larger functions, you might find yourself spending more time debugging. To deal with increasingly complex programs, you might want to try **incremental development**, which is a way of adding and testing only a small amount of code at a time.

As an example, suppose you want to find the distance between two points represented by the coordinates (x_1, y_1) and (x_2, y_2). By the Pythagorean theorem, the distance is:

$$\text{distance} = \sqrt{(x_2 - x_1)^2 + (y_2 - y_1)^2}$$

The first step is to consider what a distance function should look like in Python—that is, what are the inputs (parameters) and what is the output (return value)?

For this function, the inputs are the coordinates of the points. The return value is the distance. Immediately you can write an outline of the function:

```
def distance(x1, y1, x2, y2):
    return 0.0
```

This version doesn't compute distances yet—it always returns zero. But it is a complete function with a return value, which means that you can test it before you make it more complicated.

To test the new function, we'll call it with sample arguments:

```
distance(1, 2, 4, 6)
```

```
0.0
```

I chose these values so that the horizontal distance is 3 and the vertical distance is 4. That way, the result is 5, the hypotenuse of a 3-4-5 right triangle. When testing a function, it is useful to know the right answer.

At this point we have confirmed that the function runs and returns a value, and we can start adding code to the body. A good next step is to find the differences x2 - x1 and y2 - y1. Here's a version that stores those values in temporary variables and displays them:

```
def distance(x1, y1, x2, y2):
    dx = x2 - x1
    dy = y2 - y1
    print('dx is', dx)
    print('dy is', dy)
    return 0.0
```

If the function is working, it should display dx is 3 and dy is 4. If so, we know that the function is getting the right arguments and performing the first computation correctly. If not, there are only a few lines to check:

```
distance(1, 2, 4, 6)
```

```
dx is 3
dy is 4
```

```
0.0
```

Good so far. Next we compute the sum of squares of dx and dy:

```
def distance(x1, y1, x2, y2):
    dx = x2 - x1
    dy = y2 - y1
    dsquared = dx**2 + dy**2
    print('dsquared is: ', dsquared)
    return 0.0
```

Again, we can run the function and check the output, which should be 25:

```
distance(1, 2, 4, 6)
```

```
dsquared is:  25
```

```
0.0
```

Finally, we can use `math.sqrt` to compute the distance:

```
def distance(x1, y1, x2, y2):
    dx = x2 - x1
    dy = y2 - y1
    dsquared = dx**2 + dy**2
    result = math.sqrt(dsquared)
    print("result is", result)
```

And test it:

```
distance(1, 2, 4, 6)
```

```
result is 5.0
```

The result is correct, but this version of the function displays the result rather than returning it, so the return value is None. We can fix that by replacing the print function with a `return` statement:

```
def distance(x1, y1, x2, y2):
    dx = x2 - x1
    dy = y2 - y1
    dsquared = dx**2 + dy**2
    result = math.sqrt(dsquared)
    return result
```

This version of `distance` is a pure function. If we call it like this, only the result is displayed:

```
distance(1, 2, 4, 6)
```

```
5.0
```

And if we assign the result to a variable, nothing is displayed:

```
d = distance(1, 2, 4, 6)
```

The `print` statements we wrote are useful for debugging, but once the function is working, we can remove them. Code like that is called **scaffolding** because it is helpful for building the program but is not part of the final product. This example demonstrates incremental development. The key aspects of this process are:

1. Start with a working program, make small changes, and test after every change.
2. Use variables to hold intermediate values so you can display and check them.
3. Once the program is working, remove the scaffolding.

At any point, if there is an error, you should have a good idea where it is. Incremental development can save you a lot of debugging time.

Boolean Functions

Functions can return the boolean values `True` and `False`, which is often convenient for encapsulating a complex test in a function. For example, `is_divisible` checks whether x is divisible by y with no remainder:

```
def is_divisible(x, y):
    if x % y == 0:
        return True
    else:
        return False
```

Here's how we use it:

```
is_divisible(6, 4)
```

```
False
```

```
is_divisible(6, 3)
```

```
True
```

Inside the function, the result of the == operator is a boolean, so we can write the function more concisely by returning it directly:

```
def is_divisible(x, y):
    return x % y == 0
```

Boolean functions are often used in conditional statements:

```
if is_divisible(6, 2):
    print('divisible')
```

```
divisible
```

It might be tempting to write something like this:

```
if is_divisible(6, 2) == True:
    print('divisible')
```

```
divisible
```

But the comparison is unnecessary.

Recursion with Return Values

Now that we can write functions with return values, we can write recursive functions with return values, and with that capability, we have passed an important threshold—the subset of Python we have is now **Turing complete**, which means that we can perform any computation that can be described by an algorithm.

To demonstrate recursion with return values, we'll evaluate a few recursively defined mathematical functions. A recursive definition is similar to a circular definition, in the sense that the definition refers to the thing being defined. A truly circular definition is not very useful:

vorpal: An adjective used to describe something that is vorpal.

If you saw that definition in the dictionary, you might be annoyed. On the other hand, if you looked up the definition of the factorial function, denoted with the symbol !, you might get something like this:

$$0! = 1$$
$$n! = n \ (n-1)!$$

This definition says that the factorial of 0 is 1, and the factorial of any other value, n, is n multiplied by the factorial of $n-1$.

If you can write a recursive definition of something, you can write a Python program to evaluate it. Following an incremental development process, we'll start with a function that takes n as a parameter and always returns 0:

```
def factorial(n):
    return 0
```

Now let's add the first part of the definition—if the argument happens to be 0, all we have to do is return 1:

```
def factorial(n):
    if n == 0:
        return 1
    else:
        return 0
```

Now let's fill in the second part—if n is not 0, we have to make a recursive call to find the factorial of $n - 1$ and then multiply the result by n:

```
def factorial(n):
    if n == 0:
        return 1
    else:
        recurse = factorial(n-1)
        return n * recurse
```

The flow of execution for this program is similar to the flow of countdown in Chapter 5. If we call factorial with the value 3:

Since 3 is not 0, we take the second branch and calculate the factorial of n-1...

Since 2 is not 0, we take the second branch and calculate the factorial of n-1...

Since 1 is not 0, we take the second branch and calculate the factorial of n-1...

Since 0 equals 0, we take the first branch and return 1 without making any more recursive calls.

The return value, 1, is multiplied by n, which is 1, and the result is returned.

The return value, 1, is multiplied by n, which is 2, and the result is returned.

The return value 2 is multiplied by n, which is 3, and the result, 6, becomes the return value of the function call that started the whole process.

The following figure shows the stack diagram for this sequence of function calls:

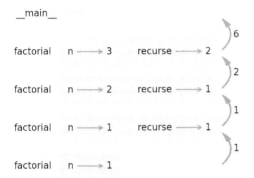

The return values are shown being passed back up the stack. In each frame, the return value is the product of n and `recurse`.

In the last frame, the local variable `recurse` does not exist because the branch that creates it does not run.

Leap of Faith

Following the flow of execution is one way to read programs, but it can quickly become overwhelming. An alternative is what I call the "leap of faith." When you come to a function call, instead of following the flow of execution, you *assume* that the function works correctly and returns the right result.

In fact, you are already practicing this leap of faith when you use built-in functions. When you call abs or math.sqrt, you don't examine the bodies of those functions—you just assume that they work.

The same is true when you call one of your own functions. For example, earlier we wrote a function called is_divisible that determines whether one number is divisible by another. Once we convince ourselves that this function is correct, we can use it without looking at the body again.

The same is true of recursive programs. When you get to the recursive call, instead of following the flow of execution, you should assume that the recursive call works and then ask yourself, "Assuming that I can compute the factorial of $n - 1$, can I compute the factorial of n?" The recursive definition of factorial implies that you can, by multiplying by n.

Of course, it's a bit strange to assume that the function works correctly when you haven't finished writing it, but that's why it's called a leap of faith!

Fibonacci

After `factorial`, the most common example of a recursive function is `fibonacci`, which has the following definition:

fibonacci(0) = 0
fibonacci(1) = 1
fibonacci(n) = fibonacci(n − 1) + fibonacci(n − 2)

Translated into Python, it looks like this:

```python
def fibonacci(n):
    if n == 0:
        return 0
    elif n == 1:
        return 1
    else:
        return fibonacci(n-1) + fibonacci(n-2)
```

If you try to follow the flow of execution here, even for small values of n, your head explodes. But according to the leap of faith, if you assume that the two recursive calls work correctly, you can be confident that the last return statement is correct.

As an aside, this way of computing Fibonacci numbers is very inefficient. In "Memos" on page 146 I'll explain why and suggest a way to improve it.

Checking Types

What happens if we call `factorial` and give it `1.5` as an argument?

```python
factorial(1.5)
```

```
RecursionError: maximum recursion depth exceeded in comparison
```

It looks like an infinite recursion. How can that be? The function has a base case—when `n == 0`. But if `n` is not an integer, we can *miss* the base case and recurse forever.

In this example, the initial value of `n` is `1.5`. In the first recursive call, the value of `n` is `0.5`. In the next, it is `-0.5`. From there, it gets smaller (more negative), but it will never be `0`.

To avoid infinite recursion we can use the built-in function `isinstance` to check the type of the argument. Here's how we check whether a value is an integer:

```
isinstance(3, int)
```

True

```
isinstance(1.5, int)
```

False

Now here's a version of `factorial` with error checking:

```
def factorial(n):
    if not isinstance(n, int):
        print('factorial is only defined for integers.')
        return None
    elif n < 0:
        print('factorial is not defined for negative numbers.')
        return None
    elif n == 0:
        return 1
    else:
        return n * factorial(n-1)
```

First, it checks whether n is an integer. If not, it displays an error message and returns None:

```
factorial('crunchy frog')
```

factorial is only defined for integers.

Then it checks whether n is negative. If so, it displays an error message and returns None:

```
factorial(-2)
```

factorial is not defined for negative numbers.

If we get past both checks, we know that n is a nonnegative integer, so we can be confident the recursion will terminate. Checking the parameters of a function to make sure they have the correct types and values is called **input validation**.

Debugging

Breaking a large program into smaller functions creates natural checkpoints for debugging. If a function is not working, there are three possibilities to consider:

- There is something wrong with the arguments the function is getting—that is, a precondition is violated.
- There is something wrong with the function—that is, a postcondition is violated.
- The caller is doing something wrong with the return value.

To rule out the first possibility, you can add a `print` statement at the beginning of the function that displays the values of the parameters (and maybe their types). Or you can write code that checks the preconditions explicitly.

If the parameters look good, you can add a `print` statement before each `return` statement and display the return value. If possible, call the function with arguments that make it easy check the result.

If the function seems to be working, look at the function call to make sure the return value is being used correctly—or used at all!

Adding `print` statements at the beginning and end of a function can help make the flow of execution more visible. For example, here is a version of `factorial` with `print` statements:

```
def factorial(n):
    space = ' ' * (4 * n)
    print(space, 'factorial', n)
    if n == 0:
        print(space, 'returning 1')
        return 1
    else:
        recurse = factorial(n-1)
        result = n * recurse
        print(space, 'returning', result)
        return result
```

`space` is a string of space characters that controls the indentation of the output. Here is the result of `factorial(4)`:

```
factorial(3)
```

```
            factorial 3
        factorial 2
    factorial 1
factorial 0
returning 1
    returning 1
        returning 2
            returning 6
```

```
6
```

If you are confused about the flow of execution, this kind of output can be helpful. It takes some time to develop effective scaffolding, but a little bit of scaffolding can save a lot of debugging.

Glossary

return value: The result of a function. If a function call is used as an expression, the return value is the value of the expression.

pure function: A function that does not display anything or have any other effect, other than returning a return value.

dead code: Part of a program that can never run, often because it appears after a return statement.

incremental development: A program development plan intended to avoid debugging by adding and testing only a small amount of code at a time.

scaffolding: Code that is used during program development but is not part of the final version.

Turing complete: A language, or subset of a language, is Turing complete if it can perform any computation that can be described by an algorithm.

input validation: Checking the parameters of a function to make sure they have the correct types and values.

Exercises

Ask a Virtual Assistant

In this chapter, we saw an incorrect function that can end without returning a value:

```
def absolute_value_wrong(x):
    if x < 0:
        return -x
    if x > 0:
        return x
```

And a version of the same function that has dead code at the end:

```
def absolute_value_extra_return(x):
    if x < 0:
        return -x
    else:
        return x

    return 'This is dead code.'
```

And we saw the following example, which is correct but not idiomatic:

```
def is_divisible(x, y):
    if x % y == 0:
        return True
    else:
        return False
```

Ask a virtual assistant what's wrong with each of these functions and see if it can spot the errors or improve the style.

Then ask "Write a function that takes coordinates of two points and computes the distance between them." See if the result resembles the version of distance we wrote in this chapter.

Exercise

Use incremental development to write a function called hypot that returns the length of the hypotenuse of a right triangle given the lengths of the other two legs as arguments.

Note that there's a function in the math module called hypot that does the same thing, but you should not use it for this exercise!

Even if you can write the function correctly on the first try, start with a function that always returns 0 and practice making small changes, testing as you go. When you are done, the function should only return a value—it should not display anything.

Exercise

Write a boolean function, is_between(x, y, z), that returns True if $x < y < z$ or if $z < y < x$, and False otherwise.

Exercise

The Ackermann function, $A(m, n)$, is defined as:

$$A(m, n) = \begin{cases} n + 1 & \text{if } m = 0 \\ A(m - 1, 1) & \text{if } m > 0 \text{ and } n = 0 \\ A(m - 1, A(m, n - 1)) & \text{if } m > 0 \text{ and } n > 0. \end{cases}$$

Write a function named ackermann that evaluates the Ackermann function. What happens if you call ackermann(5, 5)?

Exercise

The greatest common divisor (GCD) of a and b is the largest number that divides both of them with no remainder.

One way to find the GCD of two numbers is based on the observation that if r is the remainder when a is divided by b, then $gcd(a, b) = gcd(b, r)$. As a base case, we can use $gcd(a, 0) = a$.

Write a function called gcd that takes parameters a and b and returns their greatest common divisor.

CHAPTER 7

Iteration and Search

In 1939, Ernest Vincent Wright published a 50,000-word novel called *Gadsby* that does not contain the letter "e." Since "e" is the most common letter in English, writing even a few words without using it is difficult. To get a sense of how difficult, in this chapter we'll compute the fraction of English words have at least one "e."

For that, we'll use for statements to loop through the letters in a string and the words in a file, and we'll update variables in a loop to count the number of words that contain an "e." We'll use the in operator to check whether a letter appears in a word, and you'll learn a programming pattern called a "linear search."

As an exercise, you'll use these tools to solve a word puzzle called "Spelling Bee."

Loops and Strings

In Chapter 3 we saw a for loop that uses the range function to display a sequence of numbers:

```
for i in range(3):
    print(i, end=' ')
```

```
0 1 2
```

This version uses the keyword argument end, so the print function puts a space after each number rather than a newline.

We can also use a `for` loop to display the letters in a string:

```
for letter in 'Gadsby':
    print(letter, end=' ')
```

```
G a d s b y
```

Notice that I changed the name of the variable from `i` to `letter`, which provides more information about the value it refers to. The variable defined in a `for` loop is called the **loop variable**.

Now that we can loop through the letters in a word, we can check whether it contains the letter "e":

```
for letter in "Gadsby":
    if letter == 'E' or letter == 'e':
        print('This word has an "e"')
```

Before we go on, let's encapsulate that loop in a function:

```
def has_e():
    for letter in "Gadsby":
        if letter == 'E' or letter == 'e':
            print('This word has an "e"')
```

And let's make it a pure function that returns `True` if the word contains an "e" and `False` otherwise:

```
def has_e():
    for letter in "Gadsby":
        if letter == 'E' or letter == 'e':
            return True
    return False
```

We can generalize it to take the word as a parameter:

```
def has_e(word):
    for letter in word:
        if letter == 'E' or letter == 'e':
            return True
    return False
```

Now we can test it like this:

```
has_e('Gadsby')
```

```
False
```

```
has_e('Emma')
```

```
True
```

Reading the Word List

To see how many words contain an "e," we'll need a word list. The one we'll use is a list of about 114,000 official crosswords; that is, words that are considered valid in crossword puzzles and other word games.

The word list is in a file called *words.txt*, which is downloaded in the notebook for this chapter. To read it, we'll use the built-in function open, which takes the name of the file as a parameter and returns a **file object** we can use to read the file:

```
file_object = open('words.txt')
```

The file object provides a function called readline, which reads characters from the file until it gets to a newline and returns the result as a string:

```
file_object.readline()
```

```
'aa\n'
```

Notice that the syntax for calling readline is different from functions we've seen so far. That's because it is a **method**, which is a function associated with an object. In this case readline is associated with the file object, so we call it using the name of the object, the dot operator, and the name of the method.

The first word in the list is "aa," which is a type of lava. The sequence \n represents the newline character that separates this word from the next.

The file object keeps track of where it is in the file, so if you call readline again, you get the next word:

```
line = file_object.readline()
line
```

```
'aah\n'
```

To remove the newline from the end of the word, we can use `strip`, which is a method associated with strings, so we can call it like this:

```
word = line.strip()
word
```

```
'aah'
```

`strip` removes whitespace characters—including spaces, tabs, and newlines—from the beginning and end of the string.

You can also use a file object as part of a `for` loop. This program reads *words.txt* and prints each word, one per line:

```
for line in open('words.txt'):
    word = line.strip()
    print(word)
```

Now that we can read the word list, the next step is to count the words. For that, we will need the ability to update variables.

Updating Variables

As you may have discovered, it is legal to make more than one assignment to the same variable. A new assignment makes an existing variable refer to a new value (and stop referring to the old value).

For example, here is an initial assignment that creates a variable:

```
x = 5
x
```

```
5
```

And here is an assignment that changes the value of a variable:

```
x = 7
x
```

```
7
```

The following figure shows what these assignments look like in a state diagram:

The dotted arrow indicates that x no longer refers to 5. The solid arrow indicates that it now refers to 7.

A common kind of assignment is an **update**, where the new value of the variable depends on the old:

```
x = x + 1
x
```

```
8
```

This statement means "get the current value of x, add one, and assign the result back to x."

If you try to update a variable that doesn't exist, you get an error, because Python evaluates the expression on the right before it assigns a value to the variable on the left:

```
y = y + 1
```

Before you can update a variable, you have to **initialize** it, usually with a simple assignment:

```
y = 0
y = y + 1
y
```

```
1
```

Increasing the value of a variable is called an **increment**; decreasing the value is called a **decrement**.

Looping and Counting

The following program counts the number of words in the word list:

```
total = 0

for line in open('words.txt'):
    word = line.strip()
    total = total + 1
```

It starts by initializing `total` to 0. Each time through the loop, it increments `total` by 1. So when the loop exits, `total` refers to the total number of words:

```
total
```

```
113783
```

A variable like this, used to count the number of times something happens, is called a **counter**.

We can add a second counter to the program to keep track of the number of words that contain an "e":

```
total = 0
count = 0

for line in open('words.txt'):
    word = line.strip()
    total = total + 1
    if has_e(word):
        count = count + 1
```

Let's see how many words contain an "e":

```
count
```

```
76162
```

As a percentage of `total`, about two-thirds of the words use the letter "e":

```
count / total * 100
```

```
66.93618554617122
```

So you can understand why it's difficult to craft a book without using any such words.

The in Operator

The version of `has_e` we wrote in this chapter is more complicated than it needs to be. Python provides an operator, `in`, that checks whether a character appears in a string:

```
word = 'Gadsby'
'e' in word
```

```
False
```

So we can rewrite has_e like this:

```
def has_e(word):
    if 'E' in word or 'e' in word:
        return True
    else:
        return False
```

And because the conditional of the if statement has a boolean value, we can eliminate the if statement and return the boolean directly:

```
def has_e(word):
    return 'E' in word or 'e' in word
```

We can simplify this function even more using the method lower, which converts the letters in a string to lowercase. Here's an example:

```
word.lower()
```

```
'gadsby'
```

lower makes a new string—it does not modify the existing string—so the value of word is unchanged:

```
word
```

```
'Gadsby'
```

Here's how we can use lower in has_e:

```
def has_e(word):
    return 'e' in word.lower()
```

```
has_e('Gadsby')
```

```
False
```

```
has_e('Emma')
```

```
True
```

Search

Based on this simpler version of has_e, let's write a more general function called uses_any that takes a second parameter that is a string of letters. It returns True if the word uses any of the letters, and False otherwise:

```
def uses_any(word, letters):
    for letter in word.lower():
        if letter in letters.lower():
            return True
    return False
```

Here's an example where the result is True:

```
uses_any('banana', 'aeiou')
```

```
True
```

And another where it is False:

```
uses_any('apple', 'xyz')
```

```
False
```

uses_only converts word and letters to lowercase, so it works with any combination of cases:

```
uses_any('Banana', 'AEIOU')
```

```
True
```

The structure of uses_any is similar to has_e. It loops through the letters in word and checks them one at a time. If it finds one that appears in letters, it returns True immediately. If it gets all the way through the loop without finding any, it returns False.

This pattern is called a **linear search**. In the exercises at the end of this chapter, you'll write more functions that use this pattern.

Doctest

In "Docstrings" on page 48 we used a docstring to document a function—that is, to explain what it does. It is also possible to use a docstring to *test* a function. Here's a version of uses_any with a docstring that includes tests:

```
def uses_any(word, letters):
    """Checks if a word uses any of a list of letters.

    >>> uses_any('banana', 'aeiou')
    True
    >>> uses_any('apple', 'xyz')
    False
    """
    for letter in word.lower():
        if letter in letters.lower():
            return True
    return False
```

Each test begins with >>>, which is used as a prompt in some Python environments to indicate where the user can type code. In a doctest, the prompt is followed by an expression, usually a function call. The following line indicates the value the expression should have if the function works correctly.

In the first example, 'banana' uses 'a', so the result should be True. In the second example, 'apple' does not use any of 'xyz', so the result should be False.

To run these tests, we have to import the doctest module and run a function called run_docstring_examples. To make this function easier to use, I wrote the following function, which takes a function object as an argument:

```
from doctest import run_docstring_examples

def run_doctests(func):
    run_docstring_examples(func, globals(), name=func.__name__)
```

We haven't learned about globals and __name__ yet—you can ignore them. Now we can test uses_any like this:

```
run_doctests(uses_any)
```

run_doctests finds the expressions in the docstring and evaluates them. If the result is the expected value, the test **passes**. Otherwise it **fails**.

If all tests pass, run_doctests displays no output—in that case, no news is good news. To see what happens when a test fails, here's an incorrect version of uses_any:

```
def uses_any_incorrect(word, letters):
    """Checks if a word uses any of a list of letters.

    >>> uses_any_incorrect('banana', 'aeiou')
    True
    >>> uses_any_incorrect('apple', 'xyz')
    False
    """
    for letter in word.lower():
        if letter in letters.lower():
            return True
        else:
            return False    # INCORRECT!
```

And here's what happens when we test it:

```
run_doctests(uses_any_incorrect)
```

```
**********************************************************************
File "__main__", line 4, in uses_any_incorrect
Failed example:
    uses_any_incorrect('banana', 'aeiou')
Expected:
    True
Got:
    False
```

The output includes the example that failed, the value the function was expected to produce, and the value the function actually produced. If you are not sure why this test failed, you'll have a chance to debug it as an exercise.

Glossary

loop variable: A variable defined in the header of a for loop.

file object: An object that represents an open file and keeps track of which parts of the file have been read or written.

method: A function associated with an object and called using the dot operator.

update: An assignment statement that gives a new value to a variable that already exists, rather than creating a new variable.

initialize: Create a new variable and give it a value.

increment: Increase the value of a variable.

decrement: Decrease the value of a variable.

counter: A variable used to count something, usually initialized to zero and then incremented.

linear search: A computational pattern that searches through a sequence of elements and stops when it finds what it is looking for.

pass: If a test runs and the result is as expected, the test passes.

fail: If a test runs and the result is not as expected, the test fails.

Exercises

Ask a Virtual Assistant

In `uses_any`, you might have noticed that the first `return` statement is inside the loop and the second is outside:

```
def uses_any(word, letters):
    for letter in word.lower():
        if letter in letters.lower():
            return True
    return False
```

When people first write functions like this, it is a common error to put both `return` statements inside the loop, like this:

```
def uses_any_incorrect(word, letters):
    for letter in word.lower():
        if letter in letters.lower():
            return True
        else:
            return False     # INCORRECT!
```

Ask a virtual assistant what's wrong with this version.

Exercise

Write a function named `uses_none` that takes a word and a string of forbidden letters, and returns `True` if the word does not use any of the forbidden letters.

Here's an outline of the function that includes two doctests. Fill in the function so it passes these tests, and add at least one more doctest:

```
def uses_none(word, forbidden):
    """Checks whether a word avoid forbidden letters.

    >>> uses_none('banana', 'xyz')
    True
    >>> uses_none('apple', 'efg')
    False
    """
    return None
```

Exercise

Write a function called `uses_only` that takes a word and a string of letters, and that returns `True` if the word contains only letters in the string.

Here's an outline of the function that includes two doctests. Fill in the function so it passes these tests, and add at least one more doctest:

```
def uses_only(word, available):
    """Checks whether a word uses only the available letters.

    >>> uses_only('banana', 'ban')
    True
    >>> uses_only('apple', 'apl')
    False
    """
    return None
```

Exercise

Write a function called `uses_all` that takes a word and a string of letters, and that returns `True` if the word contains all of the letters in the string at least once.

Here's an outline of the function that includes two doctests. Fill in the function so it passes these tests, and add at least one more doctest.

```
def uses_all(word, required):
    """Checks whether a word uses all required letters.

    >>> uses_all('banana', 'ban')
    True
    >>> uses_all('apple', 'api')
    False
    """
    return None
```

Exercise

The *New York Times* publishes a daily puzzle called "Spelling Bee" that challenges readers to spell as many words as possible using only seven letters, where one of the letters is required. The words must have at least four letters.

For example, on the day I wrote this, the letters were ACDLORT, with R as the required letter. So "color" is an acceptable word, but "told" is not, because it does not use R, and "rat" is not because it has only three letters. Letters can be repeated, so "ratatat" is acceptable.

Write a function called `check_word` that checks whether a given word is acceptable. It should take as parameters the word to check, a string of seven available letters, and a string containing the single required letter. You can use the functions you wrote in previous exercises.

Here's an outline of the function that includes doctests. Fill in the function and then check that all tests pass:

```
def check_word(word, available, required):
    """Check whether a word is acceptable.

    >>> check_word('color', 'ACDLORT', 'R')
    True
    >>> check_word('ratatat', 'ACDLORT', 'R')
    True
    >>> check_word('rat', 'ACDLORT', 'R')
    False
    >>> check_word('told', 'ACDLORT', 'R')
    False
    >>> check_word('bee', 'ACDLORT', 'R')
    False
    """
    return False
```

According to the "Spelling Bee" rules:

- Four-letter words are worth one point each.
- Longer words earn one point per letter.
- Each puzzle includes at least one "pangram" which uses every letter. These are worth seven extra points!

Write a function called score_word that takes a word and a string of available lessons and returns its score. You can assume that the word is acceptable.

Again, here's an outline of the function with doctests:

```
def word_score(word, available):
    """Compute the score for an acceptable word.

    >>> word_score('card', 'ACDLORT')
    1
    >>> word_score('color', 'ACDLORT')
    5
    >>> word_score('cartload', 'ACDLORT')
    15
    """
    return 0
```

Exercise

You might have noticed that the functions you wrote in the previous exercises had a lot in common. In fact, they are so similar you can often use one function to write another.

For example, if a word uses none of a set forbidden letters, that means it doesn't use any. So we can write a version of uses_none like this:

```
def uses_none(word, forbidden):
    """Checks whether a word avoids forbidden letters.

    >>> uses_none('banana', 'xyz')
    True
    >>> uses_none('apple', 'efg')
    False
    >>> uses_none('', 'abc')
    True
    """
    return not uses_any(word, forbidden)
```

There is also a similarity between uses_only and uses_all that you can take advantage of. If you have a working version of uses_only, see if you can write a version of uses_all that calls uses_only.

Exercise

If you got stuck on the previous question, try asking a virtual assistant, "Given a function, uses_only, which takes two strings and checks that the first uses only the letters in the second, use it to write uses_all, which takes two strings and checks whether the first uses all the letters in the second, allowing repeats."

Use run_doctests to check the answer.

Exercise

Now let's see if we can write uses_all based on uses_any.

Ask a virtual assistant, "Given a function, uses_any, which takes two strings and checks whether the first uses any of the letters in the second, use it to write uses_all, which takes two strings and checks whether the first uses all the letters in the second, allowing repeats."

If it says it can, be sure to test the result!

CHAPTER 8

Strings and Regular Expressions

Strings are not like integers, floats, and booleans. A string is a **sequence**, which means it contains multiple values in a particular order. In this chapter we'll see how to access the values that make up a string, and we'll use functions that process strings.

We'll also use regular expressions, which are a powerful tool for finding patterns in a string and performing operations like search and replace.

As an exercise, you'll have a chance to apply these tools to a word game called Wordle.

A String Is a Sequence

A string is a sequence of characters. A **character** can be a letter (in almost any alphabet), a digit, a punctuation mark, or whitespace.

You can select a character from a string with the bracket operator. This example statement selects character number 1 from fruit and assigns it to letter:

```
fruit = 'banana'
letter = fruit[1]
```

The expression in brackets is an **index**, so called because it *indicates* which character in the sequence to select. But the result might not be what you expect:

```
letter
```

```
'a'
```

The letter with index 1 is actually the second letter of the string. An index is an offset from the beginning of the string, so the offset of the first letter is 0:

```
fruit[0]
```

```
'b'
```

You can think of 'b' as the 0th letter of 'banana'—pronounced "zero-eth."

The index in brackets can be a variable:

```
i = 1
fruit[i]
```

```
'a'
```

Or an expression that contains variables and operators:

```
fruit[i+1]
```

```
'n'
```

But the value of the index has to be an integer—otherwise you get a TypeError:

```
fruit[1.5]
```

```
TypeError: string indices must be integers
```

As we saw in Chapter 1, we can use the built-in function len to get the length of a string:

```
n = len(fruit)
n
```

```
6
```

To get the last letter of a string, you might be tempted to write this:

```
fruit[n]
```

```
IndexError: string index out of range
```

But that causes an IndexError because there is no letter in 'banana' with the index 6. Because we started counting at 0, the six letters are numbered 0 to 5. To get the last character, you have to subtract 1 from n:

```
fruit[n-1]
```

```
'a'
```

But there's an easier way. To get the last letter in a string, you can use a negative index, which counts backward from the end:

```
fruit[-1]
```

```
'a'
```

The index -1 selects the last letter, -2 selects the second to last, and so on.

String Slices

A segment of a string is called a **slice**. Selecting a slice is similar to selecting a character:

```
fruit = 'banana'
fruit[0:3]
```

```
'ban'
```

The operator [n:m] returns the part of the string from the nth character to the mth character, including the first but excluding the second. This behavior is counterintuitive, but it might help to imagine the indices pointing *between* the characters, as in this figure:

```
fruit ——→ ' b a n a n a '
          | | | | | | | |
          0 1 2 3 4 5 6
```

For example, the slice [3:6] selects the letters ana, which means that 6 is legal as part of a slice, but not legal as an index.

If you omit the first index, the slice starts at the beginning of the string:

```
fruit[:3]
```

```
'ban'
```

If you omit the second index, the slice goes to the end of the string:

```
fruit[3:]
```

```
'ana'
```

If the first index is greater than or equal to the second, the result is an **empty string**, represented by two quotation marks:

```
fruit[3:3]
```

```
''
```

An empty string contains no characters and has a length of 0.

Continuing this example, what do you think `fruit[:]` means? Try it and see.

Strings Are Immutable

It is tempting to use the [ ] operator on the left side of an assignment, with the intention of changing a character in a string, like this:

```
greeting = 'Hello, world!'
greeting[0] = 'J'
```

```
TypeError: 'str' object does not support item assignment
```

The result is a `TypeError`. In the error message, the `object` is the string and the `item` is the character we tried to assign. For now, an **object** is the same thing as a value, but we will refine that definition later.

The reason for this error is that strings are **immutable**, which means you can't change an existing string. The best you can do is create a new string that is a variation of the original:

```
new_greeting = 'J' + greeting[1:]
new_greeting
```

```
'Jello, world!'
```

This example concatenates a new first letter onto a slice of `greeting`. It has no effect on the original string:

```
greeting
```

```
'Hello, world!'
```

String Comparison

The relational operators work on strings. To see if two strings are equal, we can use the == operator:

```
word = 'banana'

if word == 'banana':
    print('All right, banana.')
```

```
All right, banana.
```

Other relational operations are useful for putting words in alphabetical order:

```
def compare_word(word):
    if word < 'banana':
        print(word, 'comes before banana.')
    elif word > 'banana':
        print(word, 'comes after banana.')
    else:
        print('All right, banana.')
```

```
compare_word('apple')
```

```
apple comes before banana.
```

Python does not handle uppercase and lowercase letters the same way people do. All the uppercase letters come before all the lowercase letters, so:

```
compare_word('Pineapple')
```

```
Pineapple comes before banana.
```

To solve this problem, we can convert strings to a standard format, such as all lowercase, before performing the comparison. Keep that in mind if you have to defend yourself against a man armed with a pineapple.

String Methods

Strings provide methods that perform a variety of useful operations. A method is similar to a function—it takes arguments and returns a value—but the syntax is different. For example, the method upper takes a string and returns a new string with all uppercase letters.

Instead of the function syntax `upper(word)`, it uses the method syntax `word.upper()`:

```
word = 'banana'
new_word = word.upper()
new_word
```

```
'BANANA'
```

This use of the dot operator specifies the name of the method, `upper`, and the name of the string to apply the method to, `word`. The empty parentheses indicate that this method takes no arguments.

A method call is called an **invocation**; in this case, we would say that we are invoking `upper` on `word`.

Writing Files

String operators and methods are useful for reading and writing text files. As an example, we'll work with the text of *Dracula*, a novel by Bram Stoker that is available from Project Gutenberg (*https://www.gutenberg.org/ebooks/345*). I've downloaded the book in a plain-text file called *pg345.txt*, which we can open for reading like this:

```
reader = open('pg345.txt')
```

In addition to the text of the book, this file contains a section at the beginning with information about the book and a section at the end with information about the license. Before we process the text, we can remove this extra material by finding the special lines at the beginning and end that begin with `'***'`.

The following function takes a line and checks whether it is one of the special lines. It uses the `startswith` method, which checks whether a string starts with a given sequence of characters:

```
def is_special_line(line):
    return line.startswith('*** ')
```

We can use this function to loop through the lines in the file and print only the special lines:

```
for line in reader:
    if is_special_line(line):
        print(line.strip())
```

```
*** START OF THE PROJECT GUTENBERG EBOOK DRACULA ***
*** END OF THE PROJECT GUTENBERG EBOOK DRACULA ***
```

Now let's create a new file, called *pg345_cleaned.txt*, that contains only the text of the book. To loop through the book again, we have to open it again for reading. And, to write a new file, we can open it for writing:

```
reader = open('pg345.txt')
writer = open('pg345_cleaned.txt', 'w')
```

open takes an optional parameter that specifies the "mode"—in this example, `'w'` indicates that we're opening the file for writing. If the file doesn't exist, it will be created; if it already exists, the contents will be replaced.

As a first step, we'll loop through the file until we find the first special line:

```
for line in reader:
    if is_special_line(line):
        break
```

The `break` statement "breaks" out of the loop—that is, it causes the loop to end immediately, before we get to the end of the file.

When the loop exits, `line` contains the special line that made the conditional true:

```
line
```

```
'*** START OF THE PROJECT GUTENBERG EBOOK DRACULA ***\n'
```

Because `reader` keeps track of where it is in the file, we can use a second loop to pick up where we left off.

The following loop reads the rest of the file, one line at a time. When it finds the special line that indicates the end of the text, it breaks out of the loop. Otherwise, it writes the line to the output file:

```
for line in reader:
    if is_special_line(line):
        break
    writer.write(line)
```

When this loop exits, `line` contains the second special line:

```
line
```

```
'*** END OF THE PROJECT GUTENBERG EBOOK DRACULA ***\n'
```

At this point `reader` and `writer` are still open, which means we could keep reading lines from `reader` or writing lines to `writer`. To indicate that we're done, we can close both files by invoking the `close` method:

```
reader.close()
writer.close()
```

To check whether this process was successful, we can read the first few lines from the new file we just created:

```
for line in open('pg345_cleaned.txt'):
    line = line.strip()
    if len(line) > 0:
        print(line)
    if line.endswith('Stoker'):
        break
```

```
DRACULA
_by_
Bram Stoker
```

The `endswith` method checks whether a string ends with a given sequence of characters.

Find and Replace

In the Icelandic translation of *Dracula* from 1901, the name of one of the characters was changed from "Jonathan" to "Thomas." To make this change in the English version, we can loop through the book, use the `replace` method to replace one name with another, and write the result to a new file.

We'll start by counting the lines in the cleaned version of the file:

```
total = 0
for line in open('pg345_cleaned.txt'):
    total += 1

total
```

```
15499
```

To see whether a line contains "Jonathan," we can use the `in` operator, which checks whether this sequence of characters appears anywhere in the line:

```
total = 0
for line in open('pg345_cleaned.txt'):
    if 'Jonathan' in line:
        total += 1

total
```

```
199
```

There are 199 lines that contain the name, but that's not quite the total number of times it appears, because it can appear more than once in a line. To get the total, we can use the count method, which returns the number of times a sequence appears in a string:

```
total = 0
    for line in open('pg345_cleaned.txt'):
        total += line.count('Jonathan')

total
```

```
200
```

Now we can replace 'Jonathan' with 'Thomas' like this:

```
writer = open('pg345_replaced.txt', 'w')

for line in open('pg345_cleaned.txt'):
    line = line.replace('Jonathan', 'Thomas')
    writer.write(line)
```

The result is a new file called *pg345_replaced.txt* that contains a version of *Dracula* where Jonathan Harker is called Thomas.

Regular Expressions

If we know exactly what sequence of characters we're looking for, we can use the in operator to find it and the replace method to replace it. But there is another tool, called a **regular expression**, that can also perform these operations—and a lot more.

To demonstrate, I'll start with a simple example and we'll work our way up. Suppose, again, that we want to find all lines that contain a particular word. For a change, let's look for references to the titular character of the book, Count Dracula. Here's a line that mentions him:

```
text = "I am Dracula; and I bid you welcome, Mr. Harker, to my house."
```

And here's the **pattern** we'll use to search:

```
pattern = 'Dracula'
```

A module called re provides functions related to regular expressions. We can import it like this and use the search function to check whether the pattern appears in the text:

```
import re

result = re.search(pattern, text)
result
```

```
<re.Match object; span=(5, 12), match='Dracula'>
```

If the pattern appears in the text, search returns a Match object that contains the results of the search. Among other information, it has a variable named string that contains the text that was searched:

```
result.string
```

```
'I am Dracula; and I bid you welcome, Mr. Harker, to my house.'
```

It also provides a function called group that returns the part of the text that matched the pattern:

```
result.group()
```

```
'Dracula'
```

And it provides a function called span that returns the index in the text where the pattern starts and ends:

```
result.span()
```

```
(5, 12)
```

If the pattern doesn't appear in the text, the return value from search is None:

```
result = re.search('Count', text)
print(result)
```

```
None
```

So we can check whether the search was successful by checking whether the result is None:

```
result == None
```

```
True
```

Putting all that together, here's a function that loops through the lines in the book until it finds one that matches the given pattern, and returns the `Match` object:

```
def find_first(pattern):
    for line in open('pg345_cleaned.txt'):
        result = re.search(pattern, line)
        if result != None:
            return result
```

We can use it to find the first mention of a character:

```
result = find_first('Harker')
result.string
```

```
'CHAPTER I. Jonathan Harker's Journal\n'
```

For this example, we didn't have to use regular expressions—we could have done the same thing more easily with the `in` operator. But regular expressions can do things the `in` operator cannot.

For example, if the pattern includes the vertical bar character, '|', it can match either the sequence on the left or the sequence on the right. Suppose we want to find the first mention of Mina Murray in the book, but we are not sure whether she is referred to by first name or last. We can use the following pattern, which matches either name:

```
pattern = r'Mina|Murray'
result = find_first(pattern)
result.string
```

```
'CHAPTER V. Letters—Lucy and Mina\n'
```

We can use a pattern like this to see how many times a character is mentioned by either name. Here's a function that loops through the book and counts the number of lines that match the given pattern:

```
def count_matches(pattern):
    count = 0
    for line in open('pg345_cleaned.txt'):
        result = re.search(pattern, line)
        if result != None:
            count += 1
    return count
```

Now let's see how many times Mina is mentioned:

```
count_matches('Mina|Murray')
```

```
229
```

The special character `'^'` matches the beginning of a string, so we can find a line that starts with a given pattern:

```
result = find_first('^Dracula')
result.string
```

```
'Dracula, jumping to his feet, said:--\n'
```

And the special character `'$'` matches the end of a string, so we can find a line that ends with a given pattern (ignoring the newline at the end):

```
result = find_first('Harker$')
result.string
```

```
"by five o'clock, we must start off; for it won't do to leave Mrs. Harker\n"
```

String Substitution

Bram Stoker was born in Ireland, and when *Dracula* was published in 1897, he was living in England. So we would expect him to use the British spelling of words like "centre" and "colour." To check, we can use the following pattern, which matches either "centre" or the American spelling "center."

```
pattern = 'cent(er|re)'
```

In this pattern, the parentheses enclose the part of the pattern the vertical bar applies to. So this pattern matches a sequence that starts with `'cent'` and ends with either `'er'` or `'re'`:

```
result = find_first(pattern)
result.string
```

```
'horseshoe of the Carpathians, as if it were the centre of some sort of\n'
```

As expected, he used the British spelling.

We can also check whether he used the British spelling of "colour." The following pattern uses the special character `'?'`, which means that the previous character is optional:

```
pattern = 'colou?r'
```

This pattern matches either "colour" with the `'u'` or "color" without it:

```
result = find_first(pattern)
line = result.string
line
```

```
'undergarment with long double apron, front, and back, of coloured stuff\n'
```

Again, as expected, he used the British spelling.

Now suppose we want to produce an edition of the book with American spellings. We can use the `sub` function in the `re` module, which does **string substitution**:

```
re.sub(pattern, 'color', line)
```

```
'undergarment with long double apron, front, and back, of colored stuff\n'
```

The first argument is the pattern we want to find and replace, the second is what we want to replace it with, and the third is the string we want to search. In the result, you can see that "colour" has been replaced with "color."

Debugging

When you are reading and writing files, debugging can be tricky. If you are working in a Jupyter notebook, you can use **shell commands** to help. For example, to display the first few lines of a file, you can use the command `!head`, like this:

```
!head pg345_cleaned.txt
```

The initial exclamation point, `!`, indicates that this is a shell command, which is not part of Python. To display the last few lines, you can use `!tail`:

```
!tail pg345_cleaned.txt
```

When you are working with large files, debugging can be difficult because there might be too much output to check by hand. A good debugging strategy is to start with just part of the file, get the program working, and then run it with the whole file.

To make a small file that contains part of a larger file, we can use `!head` again with the redirect operator, `>`, which indicates that the results should be written to a file rather than displayed:

```
!head pg345_cleaned.txt > pg345_cleaned_10_lines.txt
```

By default, !head reads the first 10 lines, but it takes an optional argument that indicates the number of lines to read:

```
!head -100 pg345_cleaned.txt > pg345_cleaned_100_lines.txt
```

This shell command reads the first 100 lines from *pg345_cleaned.txt* and writes them to a file called *pg345_cleaned_100_lines.txt*.

Note that the shell commands !head and !tail are not available on all operating systems. If they don't work for you, we can write similar functions in Python. See the first exercise at the end of this chapter for suggestions.

Glossary

sequence: An ordered collection of values where each value is identified by an integer index.

character: An element of a string, including letters, numbers, and symbols.

index: An integer value used to select an item in a sequence, such as a character in a string. In Python, indices start from 0.

slice: A part of a string specified by a range of indices.

empty string: A string that contains no characters and has length 0.

object: Something a variable can refer to. An object has a type and a value.

immutable: If the elements of an object cannot be changed, the object is immutable.

invocation: An expression—or part of an expression—that calls a method.

regular expression: A sequence of characters that defines a search pattern.

pattern: A rule that specifies the requirements a string has to meet to constitute a match.

string substitution: Replacement of a string, or part of a string, with another string.

shell command: A statement in a shell language, which is a language used to interact with an operating system.

raw string: A Python string that is preceded by the letter r, which indicates that backslashes that appear in the string should not be considered part of a special sequence.

Exercises

Ask a Virtual Assistant

In this chapter, we only scratched the surface of what regular expressions can do. To get an idea of what's possible, ask a virtual assistant, "What are the most common special characters used in Python regular expressions?"

You can also ask for a pattern that matches particular kinds of strings. For example, try asking:

- "Write a Python regular expression that matches a 10-digit phone number with hyphens."
- "Write a Python regular expression that matches a street address with a number and a street name, followed by ST or AVE."
- "Write a Python regular expression that matches a full name with any common title like Mr or Mrs, followed by any number of names beginning with capital letters, possibly with hyphens between some names."

And if you want to see something more complicated, try asking for a regular expression that matches any legal URL.

A regular expression often has the letter r before the quotation mark, which indicates that it is a **raw string**. For more information, ask a virtual assistant, "What is a raw string in Python?"

Exercise

See if you can write a function that does the same thing as the shell command !head. It should take as arguments the name of a file to read, the number of lines to read, and the name of the file to write the lines into. If the third parameter is None, it should display the lines rather than write them to a file.

Consider asking a virtual assistant for help, but if you do, tell it not to use a with statement or a try statement.

Exercise

"Wordle" is an online word game where the objective is to guess a five-letter word in six or fewer attempts. Each attempt has to be recognized as a word, not including proper nouns. After each attempt, you get information about which of the letters you guessed appear in the target word, and which ones are in the correct position.

For example, suppose the target word is MOWER and you guess TRIED. You would learn that E is in the word and in the correct position, R is in the word but not in the correct position, and T, I, and D are not in the word.

As a different example, suppose you have guessed the words SPADE and CLERK, and you've learned that E is in the word, but not in either of those positions, and none of the other letters appear in the word.

Of the words in the word list, how many could be the target word? Write a function called check_word that takes a five-letter word and checks whether it could be the target word.

You can use any of the functions from the previous chapter, like uses_any.

Exercise

Continuing the previous exercise, suppose you guess the word TOTEM and learn that the E is *still* not in the right place, but the M is. How many words are left?

Exercise

The Count of Monte Cristo is a novel by Alexandre Dumas that is considered a classic. Nevertheless, in the introduction of an English translation of the book, the writer Umberto Eco confesses that he found the book to be "one of the most badly written novels of all time."

In particular, he says it is "shameless in its repetition of the same adjective," and mentions in particular the number of times "its characters either shudder or turn pale."

To see whether his objection is valid, let's count the number of times the word pale appears in any form, including pale, pales, paled, and paleness, as well as the related word pallor. Use a single regular expression that matches all of these words and no others.

CHAPTER 9

Lists

This chapter presents one of Python's most useful built-in types, lists. You will also learn more about objects and what can happen when multiple variables refer to the same object.

In the exercises at the end of the chapter, we'll make a word list and use it to search for special words like palindromes and anagrams.

A List Is a Sequence

Like a string, a **list** is a sequence of values. In a string, the values are characters; in a list, they can be any type. The values in a list are called **elements**.

There are several ways to create a new list; the simplest is to enclose the elements in square brackets ([and]). For example, here is a list of two integers:

```
numbers = [42, 123]
```

And here's a list of three strings:

```
cheeses = ['Cheddar', 'Edam', 'Gouda']
```

The elements of a list don't have to be the same type. The following list contains a string, a float, an integer, and even another list:

```
t = ['spam', 2.0, 5, [10, 20]]
```

A list within another list is **nested**.

A list that contains no elements is called an empty list; you can create one with empty brackets, [ ]:

```
empty = []
```

The len function returns the length of a list:

```
len(cheeses)
```

```
3
```

The length of an empty list is 0.

The following figure shows the state diagram for cheeses, numbers, and empty:

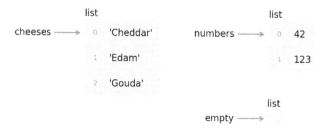

Lists are represented by boxes with the word "list" outside and the numbered elements of the list inside.

Lists Are Mutable

To read an element of a list, we can use the bracket operator. The index of the first element is 0:

```
cheeses[0]
```

```
'Cheddar'
```

Unlike strings, lists are mutable. When the bracket operator appears on the left side of an assignment, it identifies the element of the list that will be assigned:

```
numbers[1] = 17
numbers
```

```
[42, 17]
```

The second element of numbers, which used to be 123, is now 17.

List indices work the same way as string indices:

- Any integer expression can be used as an index.
- If you try to read or write an element that does not exist, you get an IndexError.
- If an index has a negative value, it counts backward from the end of the list.

The in operator works on lists—it checks whether a given element appears anywhere in the list:

```
'Edam' in cheeses
```

```
True
```

```
'Wensleydale' in cheeses
```

```
False
```

Although a list can contain another list, the nested list still counts as a single element —so in the following list, there are only four elements:

```
t = ['spam', 2.0, 5, [10, 20]]
len(t)
```

```
4
```

And 10 is not considered to be an element of t because it is an element of a nested list, not t:

```
10 in t
```

```
False
```

List Slices

The slice operator works on lists the same way it works on strings. The following example selects the second and third elements from a list of four letters:

```
letters = ['a', 'b', 'c', 'd']
letters[1:3]
```

```
['b', 'c']
```

If you omit the first index, the slice starts at the beginning:

```
letters[:2]
```

```
['a', 'b']
```

If you omit the second, the slice goes to the end:

```
letters[2:]
```

```
['c', 'd']
```

So if you omit both, the slice is a copy of the whole list:

```
letters[:]
```

```
['a', 'b', 'c', 'd']
```

Another way to copy a list is to use the `list` function:

```
list(letters)
```

```
['a', 'b', 'c', 'd']
```

Because `list` is the name of a built-in function, you should avoid using it as a variable name.

List Operations

The + operator concatenates lists:

```
t1 = [1, 2]
t2 = [3, 4]
t1 + t2
```

```
[1, 2, 3, 4]
```

The * operator repeats a list a given number of times:

```
['spam'] * 4
```

```
['spam', 'spam', 'spam', 'spam']
```

No other mathematical operators work with lists, but the built-in function `sum` adds up the elements:

```
sum(t1)
```

```
3
```

And `min` and `max` find the smallest and largest elements:

```
min(t1)
```

```
1
```

```
max(t2)
```

```
4
```

List Methods

Python provides methods that operate on lists. For example, `append` adds a new element to the end of a list:

```
letters.append('e')
letters
```

```
['a', 'b', 'c', 'd', 'e']
```

`extend` takes a list as an argument and appends all of the elements:

```
letters.extend(['f', 'g'])
letters
```

```
['a', 'b', 'c', 'd', 'e', 'f', 'g']
```

There are two methods that remove elements from a list. If you know the index of the element you want, you can use `pop`:

```
t = ['a', 'b', 'c']
t.pop(1)
```

```
'b'
```

The return value is the element that was removed. And we can confirm that the list has been modified:

```
t
```

```
['a', 'c']
```

If you know the element you want to remove (but not the index), you can use `remove`:

```
t = ['a', 'b', 'c']
t.remove('b')
```

The return value from `remove` is None. But we can confirm that the list has been modified:

```
t
```

```
['a', 'c']
```

If the element you ask for is not in the list, that's a `ValueError`:

```
t.remove('d')
```

```
ValueError: list.remove(x): x not in list
```

Lists and Strings

A string is a sequence of characters and a list is a sequence of values, but a list of characters is not the same as a string. To convert from a string to a list of characters, you can use the `list` function:

```
s = 'spam'
t = list(s)
t
```

```
['s', 'p', 'a', 'm']
```

The `list` function breaks a string into individual letters. If you want to break a string into words, you can use the `split` method:

```
s = 'pining for the fjords'
t = s.split()
t
```

```
['pining', 'for', 'the', 'fjords']
```

An optional argument called a **delimiter** specifies which characters to use as word boundaries. The following example uses a hyphen as a delimiter:

```
s = 'ex-parrot'
t = s.split('-')
t
```

```
['ex', 'parrot']
```

If you have a list of strings, you can concatenate them into a single string using join. join is a string method, so you have to invoke it on the delimiter and pass the list as an argument:

```
delimiter = ' '
t = ['pining', 'for', 'the', 'fjords']
s = delimiter.join(t)
s
```

```
'pining for the fjords'
```

In this case the delimiter is a space character, so join puts a space between words. To join strings without spaces, you can use the empty string, ' ', as a delimiter.

Looping Through a List

You can use a for statement to loop through the elements of a list:

```
for cheese in cheeses:
    print(cheese)
```

```
Cheddar
Edam
Gouda
```

For example, after using split to make a list of words, we can use for to loop through them:

```
s = 'pining for the fjords'

for word in s.split():
    print(word)
```

```
pining
for
the
fjords
```

A `for` loop over an empty list never runs the indented statements:

```
for x in []:
    print('This never happens.')
```

Sorting Lists

Python provides a built-in function called `sorted` that sorts the elements of a list:

```
scramble = ['c', 'a', 'b']
sorted(scramble)
```

```
['a', 'b', 'c']
```

The original list is unchanged:

```
scramble
```

```
['c', 'a', 'b']
```

`sorted` works with any kind of sequence, not just lists. So we can sort the letters in a string like this:

```
sorted('letters')
```

```
['e', 'e', 'l', 'r', 's', 't', 't']
```

The result is a list. To convert the list to a string, we can use `join`:

```
''.join(sorted('letters'))
```

```
'eelrstt'
```

With an empty string as the delimiter, the elements of the list are joined with nothing between them.

Objects and Values

If we run these assignment statements, we know that a and b both refer to a string, but we don't know whether they refer to the *same* string:

```
a = 'banana'
b = 'banana'
```

There are two possible states, shown in the following figure:

In the diagram on the left, a and b refer to two different objects that have the same value. In the diagram on the right, they refer to the same object. To check whether two variables refer to the same object, you can use the is operator:

```
a = 'banana'
b = 'banana'
a is b
```

```
True
```

In this example, Python only created one string object, and both a and b refer to it. But when you create two lists, you get two objects:

```
a = [1, 2, 3]
b = [1, 2, 3]
a is b
```

```
False
```

So the state diagram looks like this:

```
a ———→ [1, 2, 3]

b ———→ [1, 2, 3]
```

In this case we would say that the two lists are **equivalent** because they have the same elements, but are not **identical** because they are not the same object. If two objects are identical, they are also equivalent, but if they are equivalent, they are not necessarily identical.

Aliasing

If `a` refers to an object and you assign `b = a`, then both variables refer to the same object:

```
a = [1, 2, 3]
b = a
b is a
```

```
True
```

So the state diagram looks like this:

The association of a variable with an object is called a **reference**. In this example, there are two references to the same object.

An object with more than one reference has more than one name, so we say the object is **aliased**. If the aliased object is mutable, changes made with one name affect the other. In this example, if we change the object `b` refers to, we are also changing the object `a` refers to:

```
b[0] = 5
a
```

```
[5, 2, 3]
```

So we would say that `a` "sees" this change. Although this behavior can be useful, it is error prone. In general, it is safer to avoid aliasing when you are working with mutable objects.

For immutable objects like strings, aliasing is not as much of a problem. In this example it almost never makes a difference whether `a` and `b` refer to the same string or not:

```
a = 'banana'
b = 'banana'
```

List Arguments

When you pass a list to a function, the function gets a reference to the list. If the function modifies the list, the caller sees the change. For example, `pop_first` uses the list method `pop` to remove the first element from a list:

```
def pop_first(lst):
    return lst.pop(0)
```

We can use it like this:

```
letters = ['a', 'b', 'c']
    pop_first(letters)
```

```
'a'
```

The return value is the first element, which has been removed from the list—as we can see by displaying the modified list:

```
letters
```

```
['b', 'c']
```

In this example, the parameter `lst` and the variable `letters` are aliases for the same object, so the stack diagram looks like this:

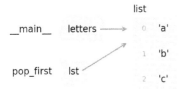

Passing a reference to an object as an argument to a function creates a form of aliasing. If the function modifies the object, those changes persist after the function is done.

Making a Word List

In the previous chapter, we read the file *words.txt* and searched for words with certain properties, like using the letter e. But we read the entire file many times, which is not efficient. It is better to read the file once and put the words in a list. The following loop shows how:

```
word_list = []

for line in open('words.txt'):
    word = line.strip()
    word_list.append(word)

len(word_list)
```

113783

Before the loop, `word_list` is initialized with an empty list. Each time through the loop, the `append` method adds a word to the end. When the loop is done, there are more than 113,000 words in the list.

Another way to do the same thing is to use `read` to read the entire file into a string:

```
string = open('words.txt').read()
len(string)
```

1016511

The result is a single string with more than a million characters. We can use the `split` method to split it into a list of words:

```
word_list = string.split()
len(word_list)
```

113783

Now, to check whether a string appears in the list, we can use the `in` operator. For example, `'demotic'` is in the list:

```
'demotic' in word_list
```

True

But `'contrafibularities'` is not:

```
'contrafibularities' in word_list
```

False

And I have to say, I'm anaspeptic about it.

Debugging

Note that most list methods modify the argument and return None. This is the opposite of the string methods, which return a new string and leave the original alone.

If you are used to writing string code like this:

```
word = 'plumage!'
word = word.strip('!')
word
```

```
'plumage'
```

It is tempting to write list code like this:

```
t = [1, 2, 3]
t = t.remove(3)          # WRONG!
```

remove modifies the list and returns None, so the next operation you perform with t is likely to fail:

```
t.remove(2)
```

```
AttributeError: 'NoneType' object has no attribute 'remove'
```

This error message takes some explaining. An **attribute** of an object is a variable or method associated with it. In this case, the value of t is None, which is a NoneType object, which does not have an attribute named remove, so the result is an AttributeError.

If you see an error message like this, you should look backward through the program and see if you might have called a list method incorrectly.

Glossary

list: An object that contains a sequence of values.

element: One of the values in a list or other sequence.

nested list: A list that is an element of another list.

delimiter: A character or string used to indicate where a string should be split.

equivalent: Having the same value.

identical: Being the same object (which implies equivalence).

reference: The association between a variable and its value.

aliased: If there is more than one variable that refers to an object, the object is aliased.

attribute: One of the named values associated with an object.

Exercises

Ask a Virtual Assistant

In this chapter, I used the words "contrafibularities" and "anaspeptic," but they are not actually English words. They are used in the British television show *Black Adder*, Season 2, Episode 2, "Ink and Incapability."

However, when I asked ChatGPT 3.5 (August 3, 2023 version) where those words come from, it initially claimed they are from Monty Python, and later claimed they are from the Tom Stoppard play *Rosencrantz and Guildenstern Are Dead*.

If you ask now, you might get different results. But this example is a reminder that virtual assistants are not always accurate, so you should check whether the results are correct. As you gain experience, you will get a sense of which questions virtual assistants can answer reliably. In this example, a conventional web search can quickly identify the source of these words.

If you get stuck on any of the exercises in this chapter, consider asking a virtual assistant for help. If you get a result that uses features we haven't learned yet, you can assign the VA a "role."

For example, before you ask a question try typing "Role: Basic Python Programming Instructor." Then the responses you get should use only basic features. If you still see features you haven't learned, you can follow up with "Can you write that using only basic Python features?"

Exercise

Two words are anagrams if you can rearrange the letters from one to spell the other. For example, `tops` is an anagram of `stop`. One way to check whether two words are anagrams is to sort the letters in both words. If the lists of sorted letters are the same, the words are anagrams.

Write a function called `is_anagram` that takes two strings and returns `True` if they are anagrams. Using your function and the word list, find all the anagrams of `takes`.

Exercise

Python provides a built-in function called `reversed` that takes as an argument a sequence of elements—like a list or string—and returns a `reversed` object that contains the elements in reverse order:

```
reversed('parrot')
```

```
<reversed at 0x7fe3de636b60>
```

If you want the reversed elements in a list, you can use the `list` function:

```
list(reversed('parrot'))
```

```
['t', 'o', 'r', 'r', 'a', 'p']
```

Or if you want them in a string, you can use the `join` method:

```
''.join(reversed('parrot'))
```

```
'torrap'
```

So we can write a function that reverses a word like this:

```
def reverse_word(word):
    return ''.join(reversed(word))
```

A palindrome is a word that is spelled the same backward and forward, like "noon" and "rotator." Write a function called `is_palindrome` that takes a string argument and returns `True` if it is a palindrome and `False` otherwise.

You can use the following loop to find all of the palindromes in the word list with at least seven letters:

```
for word in word_list:
    if len(word) >= 7 and is_palindrome(word):
        print(word)
```

Exercise

Write a function called `reverse_sentence` that takes as an argument a string that contains any number of words separated by spaces. It should return a new string that contains the same words in reverse order. For example, if the argument is "Reverse this sentence," the result should be "Sentence this reverse."

Hint: you can use the `capitalize` methods to capitalize the first word and convert the other words to lowercase.

Exercise

Write a function called `total_length` that takes a list of strings and returns the total length of the strings. The total length of the words in `word_list` should be 902,728.

CHAPTER 10

Dictionaries

This chapter presents a built-in type called a dictionary. It is one of Python's best features—and the building block of many efficient and elegant algorithms.

We'll use dictionaries to compute the number of unique words in a book and the number of times each one appears. And in the exercises, we'll use dictionaries to solve word puzzles.

A Dictionary Is a Mapping

A **dictionary** is like a list, but more general. In a list, the indices have to be integers; in a dictionary they can be (almost) any type. For example, suppose we make a list of number words, like this:

```
lst = ['zero', 'one', 'two']
```

We can use an integer as an index to get the corresponding word:

```
lst[1]
```

```
'one'
```

But suppose we want to go in the other direction, and look up a word to get the corresponding integer. We can't do that with a list, but we can with a dictionary. We'll start by creating an empty dictionary and assigning it to `numbers`:

```
numbers = {}
numbers
```

```
{}
```

The curly braces, {}, represent an empty dictionary. To add items to the dictionary, we'll use square brackets:

```
numbers['zero'] = 0
```

This assignment adds to the dictionary an **item**, which represents the association of a **key** and a **value**. In this example, the key is the string `'zero'` and the value is the integer `0`. If we display the dictionary, we see that it contains one item, which contains a key and a value separated by a colon:

```
numbers
```

```
{'zero': 0}
```

We can add more items like this:

```
numbers['one'] = 1
numbers['two'] = 2
numbers
```

```
{'zero': 0, 'one': 1, 'two': 2}
```

Now the dictionary contains three items.

To look up a key and get the corresponding value, we use the bracket operator:

```
numbers['two']
```

```
2
```

If the key isn't in the dictionary, we get a KeyError:

```
numbers['three']
```

```
KeyError: 'three'
```

The len function works on dictionaries; it returns the number of items:

```
len(numbers)
```

```
3
```

In mathematical language, a dictionary represents a **mapping** from keys to values, so you can also say that each key "maps to" a value. In this example, each number word maps to the corresponding integer.

The following figure shows the state diagram for `numbers`:

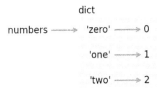

A dictionary is represented by a box with the word `dict` outside and the items inside. Each item is represented by a key and an arrow pointing to a value. The quotation marks indicate that the keys here are strings, not variable names.

Creating Dictionaries

In the previous section we created an empty dictionary and added items one at a time using the bracket operator. Instead, we could have created the dictionary all at once like this:

```
numbers = {'zero': 0, 'one': 1, 'two': 2}
```

Each item consists of a key and a value separated by a colon. The items are separated by commas and enclosed in curly braces.

Another way to create a dictionary is to use the `dict` function. We can make an empty dictionary like this:

```
empty = dict()
empty
```

```
{}
```

And we can make a copy of a dictionary like this:

```
numbers_copy = dict(numbers)
numbers_copy
```

```
{'zero': 0, 'one': 1, 'two': 2}
```

It is often useful to make a copy before performing operations that modify dictionaries.

The in Operator

The `in` operator works on dictionaries, too; it tells you whether something appears as a *key* in the dictionary:

```
'one' in numbers
```

```
True
```

The `in` operator does *not* check whether something appears as a value:

```
1 in numbers
```

```
False
```

To see whether something appears as a value in a dictionary, you can use the method `values`, which returns a sequence of values, and then use the `in` operator:

```
1 in numbers.values()
```

```
True
```

The items in a Python dictionary are stored in a **hash table**, which is a way of organizing data that has a remarkable property: the `in` operator takes about the same amount of time no matter how many items are in the dictionary. That makes it possible to write some remarkably efficient algorithms.

To demonstrate, we'll compare two algorithms for finding pairs of words where one is the reverse of another—like `stressed` and `desserts`. We'll start by reading the word list:

```
word_list = open('words.txt').read().split()
len(word_list)
```

```
113783
```

And here's `reverse_word` from the previous chapter:

```
def reverse_word(word):
    return ''.join(reversed(word))
```

The following function loops through the words in the list. For each one, it reverses the letters and then checks whether the reversed word is in the word list:

```
def too_slow():
    count = 0
    for word in word_list:
        if reverse_word(word) in word_list:
            count += 1
    return count
```

This function takes more than a minute to run. The problem is that the in operator checks the words in the list one at a time, starting at the beginning. If it doesn't find what it's looking for—which happens most of the time—it has to search all the way to the end.

The in operator is inside the loop, so it runs once for each word. Since there are more than 100,000 words in the list, and for each one we check more than 100,000 words, the total number of comparisons is the number of words squared—roughly—which is almost 13 billion:

```
len(word_list)**2
```

```
12946571089
```

We can make this function much faster with a dictionary. The following loop creates a dictionary that contains the words as keys:

```
word_dict = {}
    for word in word_list:
        word_dict[word] = 1
```

The values in word_dict are all 1, but they could be anything, because we won't ever look them up—we will only use this dictionary to check whether a key exists.

Now here's a version of the previous function that replaces word_list with word_dict:

```
def much_faster():
    count = 0
    for word in word_dict:
        if reverse_word(word) in word_dict:
            count += 1
    return count
```

This function takes less than one hundredth of a second, so it's about 10,000 times faster than the previous version.

In general, the time it takes to find an element in a list is proportional to the length of the list. The time it takes to find a key in a dictionary is almost constant—regardless of the number of items:

```
d = {'a': 1, 'b': 2}
d['a'] = 3
d
```

```
{'a': 3, 'b': 2}
```

A Collection of Counters

Suppose you are given a string and you want to count how many times each letter appears. A dictionary is a good tool for this job. We'll start with an empty dictionary:

```
counter = {}
```

As we loop through the letters in the string, suppose we see the letter 'a' for the first time. We can add it to the dictionary like this:

```
counter['a'] = 1
```

The value 1 indicates that we have seen the letter once. Later, if we see the same letter again, we can increment the counter like this:

```
counter['a'] += 1
```

Now the value associated with 'a' is 2, because we've seen the letter twice:

```
counter
```

```
{'a': 2}
```

The following function uses these features to count the number of times each letter appears in a string:

```
def value_counts(string):
    counter = {}
    for letter in string:
        if letter not in counter:
            counter[letter] = 1
        else:
            counter[letter] += 1
    return counter
```

Each time through the loop, if `letter` is not in the dictionary, we create a new item with key `letter` and value 1. If `letter` is already in the dictionary we increment the value associated with `letter`. Here's an example:

```
counter = value_counts('brontosaurus')
counter
```

```
{'b': 1, 'r': 2, 'o': 2, 'n': 1, 't': 1, 's': 2, 'a': 1, 'u': 2}
```

The items in `counter` show that the letter `'b'` appears once, `'r'` appears twice, and so on.

Looping and Dictionaries

If you use a dictionary in a `for` statement, it traverses the keys of the dictionary. To demonstrate, let's make a dictionary that counts the letters in `'banana'`:

```
counter = value_counts('banana')
counter
```

```
{'b': 1, 'a': 3, 'n': 2}
```

The following loop prints the keys, which are the letters:

```
for key in counter:
    print(key)
```

```
b
a
n
```

To print the values, we can use the `values` method:

```
for value in counter.values():
    print(value)
```

```
1
3
2
```

To print the keys and values, we can loop through the keys and look up the corresponding values:

```
for key in counter:
    value = counter[key]
    print(key, value)
```

```
b 1
a 3
n 2
```

In Chapter 11, we'll see a more concise way to do the same thing.

Lists and Dictionaries

You can put a list in a dictionary as a value. For example, here's a dictionary that maps from the number 4 to a list of four letters:

```
d = {4: ['r', 'o', 'u', 's']}
d
```

```
{4: ['r', 'o', 'u', 's']}
```

But you can't put a list in a dictionary as a key. Here's what happens if we try:

```
letters = list('abcd')
d[letters] = 4
```

```
TypeError: unhashable type: 'list'
```

I mentioned earlier that dictionaries use hash tables, and that means that the keys have to be **hashable**.

A **hash** is a function that takes a value (of any kind) and returns an integer. Dictionaries use these integers, called hash values, to store and look up keys.

This system only works if a key is immutable, so its hash value is always the same. But if a key is mutable, its hash value could change, and the dictionary would not work. That's why keys have to be hashable, and why mutable types like lists aren't.

Since dictionaries are mutable, they can't be used as keys either. But they *can* be used as values.

Accumulating a List

For many programming tasks, it is useful to loop through one list or dictionary while building another. As an example, we'll loop through the words in word_dict and make a list of palindromes—that is, words that are spelled the same backward and forward, like "noon" and "rotator."

In the previous chapter, one of the exercises asked you to write a function that checks whether a word is a palindrome. Here's a solution that uses `reverse_word`:

```
def is_palindrome(word):
    """Check if a word is a palindrome."""
    return reverse_word(word) == word
```

If we loop through the words in `word_dict`, we can count the number of palindromes like this:

```
count = 0

for word in word_dict:
    if is_palindrome(word):
        count +=1

count
```

91

By now, this pattern is familiar.

- Before the loop, `count` is initialized to 0.
- Inside the loop, if `word` is a palindrome, we increment `count`.
- When the loop ends, `count` contains the total number of palindromes.

We can use a similar pattern to make a list of palindromes:

```
palindromes = []

for word in word_dict:
    if is_palindrome(word):
        palindromes.append(word)

palindromes[:10]
```

```
['aa', 'aba', 'aga', 'aha', 'ala', 'alula', 'ama', 'ana', 'anna', 'ava']
```

Here's how it works:

- Before the loop, `palindromes` is initialized with an empty list.
- Inside the loop, if `word` is a palindrome, we append it to the end of `palindromes`.
- When the loop ends, `palindromes` is a list of palindromes.

In this loop, `palindromes` is used as an **accumulator**, which is a variable that collects or accumulates data during a computation.

Now suppose we want to select only palindromes with seven or more letters. We can loop through `palindromes` and make a new list that contains only long palindromes:

```
long_palindromes = []

for word in palindromes:
    if len(word) >= 7:
        long_palindromes.append(word)

long_palindromes
```

```
['deified', 'halalah', 'reifier', 'repaper', 'reviver', 'rotator', 'sememes']
```

Looping through a list like this, selecting some elements and omitting others, is called **filtering**.

Memos

If you ran the `fibonacci` function from "Fibonacci" on page 84, maybe you noticed that the bigger the argument you provide, the longer the function takes to run:

```
def fibonacci(n):
    if n == 0:
        return 0

    if n == 1:
        return 1

    return fibonacci(n-1) + fibonacci(n-2)
```

Furthermore, the run time increases quickly. To understand why, consider the following figure, which shows the **call graph** for `fibonacci` with n=3:

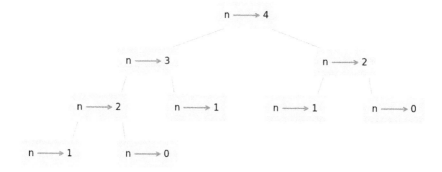

A call graph shows a set of function frames, with lines connecting each frame to the frames of the functions it calls. At the top of the graph, fibonacci with n=4 calls fibonacci with n=3 and n=2. In turn, fibonacci with n=3 calls fibonacci with n=2 and n=1. And so on.

Count how many times fibonacci(0) and fibonacci(1) are called. This is an inefficient solution to the problem, and it gets worse as the argument gets bigger.

One solution is to keep track of values that have already been computed by storing them in a dictionary. A previously computed value that is stored for later use is called a **memo**. Here is a "memoized" version of fibonacci:

```
known = {0:0, 1:1}

def fibonacci_memo(n):
    if n in known:
        return known[n]

    res = fibonacci_memo(n-1) + fibonacci_memo(n-2)
    known[n] = res
    return res
```

known is a dictionary that keeps track of the Fibonacci numbers we already know. It starts with two items: 0 maps to 0, and 1 maps to 1.

Whenever fibonacci_memo is called, it checks known. If the result is already there, it can return immediately. Otherwise it has to compute the new value, add it to the dictionary, and return it.

Comparing the two functions, fibonacci(40) takes about 30 seconds to run. fibonacci_memo(40) takes about 30 microseconds, so it's a million times faster. In the notebook for this chapter, you'll see where these measurements come from.

Debugging

As you work with bigger datasets it can become unwieldy to debug by printing and checking the output by hand. Here are some suggestions for debugging large datasets:

Scale down the input

If possible, reduce the size of the dataset. For example, if the program reads a text file, start with just the first 10 lines, or with the smallest example you can find. You can either edit the files, or (better) modify the program so it reads only the first n lines.

If there is an error, you can reduce n to the smallest value where the error occurs. As you find and correct errors, you can increase n gradually.

Check summaries and types

Instead of printing and checking the entire dataset, consider printing summaries of the data—for example, the number of items in a dictionary or the total of a list of numbers.

A common cause of runtime errors is a value that is not the right type. For debugging this kind of error, it is often enough to print the type of a value.

Write self-checks

Sometimes you can write code to check for errors automatically. For example, if you are computing the average of a list of numbers, you could check that the result is not greater than the largest element in the list or less than the smallest. This is called a "sanity check" because it detects results that are "insane."

Another kind of check compares the results of two different computations to see if they are consistent. This is called a "consistency check."

Format the output

Formatting debugging output can make it easier to spot an error. We saw an example in "Debugging" on page 85. Another tool you might find useful is the pprint module, which provides a pprint function that displays built-in types in a more human-readable format (pprint stands for "pretty print").

Again, time you spend building scaffolding can reduce the time you spend debugging.

Glossary

dictionary: An object that contains key-value pairs, also called items.

item: In a dictionary, another name for a key-value pair.

key: An object that appears in a dictionary as the first part of a key-value pair.

value: An object that appears in a dictionary as the second part of a key-value pair. This is more specific than our previous use of the word "value."

mapping: A relationship in which each element of one set corresponds to an element of another set.

hash table: A collection of key-value pairs organized so that we can look up a key and find its value efficiently.

hashable: Immutable types like integers, floats, and strings are hashable. Mutable types like lists and dictionaries are not.

hash function: A function that takes an object and computes an integer that is used to locate a key in a hash table.

accumulator: A variable used in a loop to add up or accumulate a result.

filtering: Looping through a sequence and selecting or omitting elements.

call graph: A diagram that shows every frame created during the execution of a program, with an arrow from each caller to each callee.

memo: A computed value stored to avoid unnecessary future computation.

Exercises

Ask a Virtual Assistant

In this chapter, I said the keys in a dictionary have to be hashable and I gave a short explanation. If you would like more details, ask a virtual assistant, "Why do keys in Python dictionaries have to be hashable?"

In "The in Operator" on page 140, we stored a list of words as keys in a dictionary so that we could use an efficient version of the in operator. We could have done the same thing using a set, which is another built-in data type. Ask a virtual assistant, "How do I make a Python set from a list of strings and check whether a string is an element of the set?"

Exercise

Dictionaries have a method called get that takes a key and a default value. If the key appears in the dictionary, get returns the corresponding value; otherwise it returns the default value. For example, here's a dictionary that maps from the letters in a string to the number of times they appear:

```
counter = value_counts('brontosaurus')
```

If we look up a letter that appears in the word, get returns the number of times it appears:

```
counter.get('b', 0)
```

```
1
```

If we look up a letter that doesn't appear, we get the default value, 0:

```
counter.get('c', 0)
```

```
0
```

Use `get` to write a more concise version of `value_counts`. You should be able to eliminate the `if` statement.

Exercise

What is the longest word you can think of where each letter appears only once? Let's see if we can find one longer than `unpredictably`.

Write a function named `has_duplicates` that takes a sequence—like a list or string—as a parameter and returns `True` if there is any element that appears in the sequence more than once.

Exercise

Write a function called `find_repeats` that takes a dictionary that maps from each key to a counter, like the result from `value_counts`. It should loop through the dictionary and return a list of keys that have counts greater than 1. You can use the following outline to get started:

```
def find_repeats(counter):
    """Makes a list of keys with values greater than 1.

    counter: dictionary that maps from keys to counts

    returns: list of keys
    """
    return []
```

Exercise

Suppose you run `value_counts` with two different words and save the results in two dictionaries:

```
counter1 = value_counts('brontosaurus')
counter2 = value_counts('apatosaurus')
```

Each dictionary maps from a set of letters to the number of times they appear. Write a function called `add_counters` that takes two dictionaries like this and returns a new dictionary that contains all of the letters and the total number of times they appear in either word.

There are many ways to solve this problem. Once you have a working solution, consider asking a virtual assistant for different solutions.

Exercise

A word is "interlocking" if we can split it into two words by taking alternating letters. For example, "schooled" is an interlocking word because it can be split into "shoe" and "cold."

To select alternating letters from a string, you can use a slice operator with three components that indicate where to start, where to stop, and the "step size" between the letters.

In the following slice, the first component is 0, so we start with the first letter. The second component is None, which means we should go all the way to the end of the string. And the third component is 2, so there are two steps between the letters we select:

```
word = 'schooled'
first = word[0:None:2]
first
```

```
'shoe'
```

Instead of providing None as the second component, we can get the same effect by leaving it out altogether. For example, the following slice selects alternating letters, starting with the second letter:

```
second = word[1::2]
second
```

```
'cold'
```

Write a function called is_interlocking that takes a word as an argument and returns True if it can be split into two interlocking words.

CHAPTER 11

Tuples

This chapter introduces one more built-in type, the tuple, and then shows how lists, dictionaries, and tuples work together. It also presents tuple assignment and a useful feature for functions with variable-length argument lists: the packing and unpacking operators.

In the exercises, we'll use tuples, along with lists and dictionaries, to solve more word puzzles and implement efficient algorithms.

One note: there are two ways to pronounce "tuple." Some people say "tuh-ple," which rhymes with "supple." But in the context of programming, most people say "too-ple," which rhymes with "quadruple."

Tuples Are Like Lists

A **tuple** is a sequence of values. The values can be any type, and they are indexed by integers, so tuples are a lot like lists. The important difference is that tuples are immutable.

To create a tuple, you can write a comma-separated list of values:

```
t = 'l', 'u', 'p', 'i', 'n'
type(t)
```

```
tuple
```

Although it is not necessary, it is common to enclose tuples in parentheses:

```
t = ('l', 'u', 'p', 'i', 'n')
type(t)
```

```
tuple
```

To create a tuple with a single element, you have to include a final comma:

```
t1 = 'p',
type(t1)
```

```
tuple
```

A single value in parentheses is not a tuple:

```
t2 = ('p')
type(t2)
```

```
str
```

Another way to create a tuple is the built-in function `tuple`. With no argument, it creates an empty tuple:

```
t = tuple()
t
```

```
()
```

If the argument is a sequence (string, list, or tuple), the result is a tuple with the elements of the sequence:

```
t = tuple('lupin')
t
```

```
('l', 'u', 'p', 'i', 'n')
```

Because `tuple` is the name of a built-in function, you should avoid using it as a variable name.

Most list operators also work with tuples. For example, the bracket operator indexes an element:

```
t[0]
```

```
'l'
```

And the slice operator selects a range of elements:

```
t[1:3]
```

```
('u', 'p')
```

The + operator concatenates tuples:

```
tuple('lup') + ('i', 'n')
```

```
('l', 'u', 'p', 'i', 'n')
```

And the * operator duplicates a tuple a given number of times:

```
tuple('spam') * 2
```

```
('s', 'p', 'a', 'm', 's', 'p', 'a', 'm')
```

The sorted function works with tuples—but the result is a list, not a tuple:

```
sorted(t)
```

```
['i', 'l', 'n', 'p', 'u']
```

The reversed function also works with tuples:

```
reversed(t)
```

```
<reversed at 0x7f56c0072110>
```

The result is a reversed object, which we can convert to a list or tuple:

```
tuple(reversed(t))
```

```
('n', 'i', 'p', 'u', 'l')
```

Based on the examples so far, it might seem like tuples are the same as lists.

But Tuples Are Immutable

If you try to modify a tuple with the bracket operator, you get a TypeError:

```
t[0] = 'L'
```

```
TypeError: 'tuple' object does not support item assignment
```

And tuples don't have any of the methods that modify lists, like append and remove:

```
t.remove('l')
```

```
AttributeError: 'tuple' object has no attribute 'remove'
```

Recall that an "attribute" is a variable or method associated with an object—this error message means that tuples don't have a method named remove.

Because tuples are immutable, they are hashable, which means they can be used as keys in a dictionary. For example, the following dictionary contains two tuples as keys that map to integers:

```
d = {}
d[1, 2] = 3
d[3, 4] = 7
```

We can look up a tuple in a dictionary like this:

```
d[1, 2]
```

```
3
```

Or if we have a variable that refers to a tuple, we can use it as a key:

```
t = (3, 4)
d[t]
```

```
7
```

Tuples can also appear as values in a dictionary:

```
t = tuple('abc')
s = [1, 2, 3]
d = {t: s}
d
```

```
{('a', 'b', 'c'): [1, 2, 3]}
```

Tuple Assignment

You can put a tuple of variables on the left side of an assignment, and a tuple of values on the right:

```
a, b = 1, 2
```

The values are assigned to the variables from left to right—in this example, a gets the value 1, and b gets the value 2. We can display the results like this:

```
a, b
```

```
(1, 2)
```

More generally, if the left side of an assignment is a tuple, the right side can be any kind of sequence—string, list, or tuple. For example, to split an email address into a username and a domain, you could write:

```
email = 'monty@python.org'
username, domain = email.split('@')
```

The return value from split is a list with two elements—the first element is assigned to username, the second to domain:

```
username, domain
```

```
('monty', 'python.org')
```

The number of variables on the left and the number of values on the right have to be the same—otherwise you get a ValueError:

```
a, b = 1, 2, 3
```

```
ValueError: too many values to unpack (expected 2)
```

Tuple assignment is useful if you want to swap the values of two variables. With conventional assignments, you have to use a temporary variable, like this:

```
temp = a
a = b
b = temp
```

That works, but with tuple assignment we can do the same thing without a temporary variable:

```
a, b = b, a
```

This works because all of the expressions on the right side are evaluated before any of the assignments.

We can also use tuple assignment in a `for` statement. For example, to loop through the items in a dictionary, we can use the `items` method:

```
d = {'one': 1, 'two': 2}

for item in d.items():
    key, value = item
    print(key, '->', value)
```

```
one -> 1
two -> 2
```

Each time through the loop, `item` is assigned a tuple that contains a key and the corresponding value.

We can write this loop more concisely, like this:

```
for key, value in d.items():
    print(key, '->', value)
```

```
one -> 1
two -> 2
```

Each time through the loop, a key and the corresponding value are assigned directly to `key` and `value`.

Tuples as Return Values

Strictly speaking, a function can only return one value, but if the value is a tuple, the effect is the same as returning multiple values. For example, if you want to divide two integers and compute the quotient and remainder, it is inefficient to compute `x//y` and then `x%y`. It is better to compute them both at the same time.

The built-in function `divmod` takes two arguments and returns a tuple of two values, the quotient and remainder:

```
divmod(7, 3)
```

```
(2, 1)
```

We can use tuple assignment to store the elements of the tuple in two variables:

```
quotient, remainder = divmod(7, 3)
quotient
```

```
2
```

remainder
1

Here is an example of a function that returns a tuple:

```
def min_max(t):
    return min(t), max(t)
```

`max` and `min` are built-in functions that find the largest and smallest elements of a sequence. `min_max` computes both and returns a tuple of two values:

```
min_max([2, 4, 1, 3])
```

```
(1, 4)
```

We can assign the results to variables like this:

```
low, high = min_max([2, 4, 1, 3])
low, high
```

```
(1, 4)
```

Argument Packing

Functions can take a variable number of arguments. A parameter name that begins with the * operator **packs** arguments into a tuple. For example, the following function takes any number of arguments and computes their arithmetic mean—that is, their sum divided by the number of arguments:

```
def mean(*args):
    return sum(args) / len(args)
```

The parameter can have any name you like, but `args` is conventional. We can call the function like this:

```
mean(1, 2, 3)
```

```
2.0
```

If you have a sequence of values and you want to pass them to a function as multiple arguments, you can use the * operator to **unpack** the tuple. For example, `divmod` takes exactly two arguments—if you pass a tuple as a parameter, you get an error:

```
t = (7, 3)
divmod(t)
```

```
TypeError: divmod expected 2 arguments, got 1
```

Even though the tuple contains two elements, it counts as a single argument. But if you unpack the tuple, it is treated as two arguments:

```
divmod(*t)
```

```
(2, 1)
```

Packing and unpacking can be useful if you want to adapt the behavior of an existing function. For example, this function takes any number of arguments, removes the lowest and highest, and computes the mean of the rest:

```
def trimmed_mean(*args):
    low, high = min_max(args)
    trimmed = list(args)
    trimmed.remove(low)
    trimmed.remove(high)
    return mean(*trimmed)
```

First, it uses min_max to find the lowest and highest elements. Then it converts args to a list so it can use the remove method. Finally, it unpacks the list so the elements are passed to mean as separate arguments, rather than as a single list.

Here's an example that shows the effect:

```
mean(1, 2, 3, 10)
```

```
4.0
```

```
trimmed_mean(1, 2, 3, 10)
```

```
2.5
```

This kind of "trimmed" mean is used in some sports with subjective judging—like diving and gymnastics—to reduce the effect of a judge whose score deviates from the others.

Zip

Tuples are useful for looping through the elements of two sequences and performing operations on corresponding elements. For example, suppose two teams play a series of seven games, and we record their scores in two lists, one for each team:

```
scores1 = [1, 2, 4, 5, 1, 5, 2]
scores2 = [5, 5, 2, 2, 5, 2, 3]
```

Let's see how many games each team won. We'll use `zip`, which is a built-in function that takes two or more sequences and returns a **zip object**, so-called because it pairs up the elements of the sequences like the teeth of a zipper:

```
zip(scores1, scores2)
```

```
<zip at 0x7f3e9c74f0c0>
```

We can use the zip object to loop through the values in the sequences pairwise:

```
for pair in zip(scores1, scores2):
    print(pair)
```

```
(1, 5)
(2, 5)
(4, 2)
(5, 2)
(1, 5)
(5, 2)
(2, 3)
```

Each time through the loop, `pair` gets assigned a tuple of scores. So we can assign the scores to variables, and count the victories for the first team, like this:

```
wins = 0
for team1, team2 in zip(scores1, scores2):
    if team1 > team2:
        wins += 1

wins
```

```
3
```

Sadly, the first team won only three games and lost the series.

If you have two lists and you want a list of pairs, you can use `zip` and `list`:

```
t = list(zip(scores1, scores2))
t
```

```
[(1, 5), (2, 5), (4, 2), (5, 2), (1, 5), (5, 2), (2, 3)]
```

The result is a list of tuples, so we can get the result of the last game like this:

```
t[-1]
```

```
(2, 3)
```

If you have a list of keys and a list of values, you can use `zip` and `dict` to make a dictionary. For example, here's how we can make a dictionary that maps from each letter to its position in the alphabet:

```
letters = 'abcdefghijklmnopqrstuvwxyz'
numbers = range(len(letters))
letter_map = dict(zip(letters, numbers))
```

Now we can look up a letter and get its index in the alphabet:

```
letter_map['a'], letter_map['z']
```

```
(0, 25)
```

In this mapping, the index of `'a'` is 0, and the index of `'z'` is 25.

If you need to loop through the elements of a sequence and their indices, you can use the built-in function `enumerate`:

```
enumerate('abc')
```

```
<enumerate at 0x7f3e9c620cc0>
```

The result is an **enumerate object** that loops through a sequence of pairs, where each pair contains an index (starting from 0) and an element from the given sequence:

```
for index, element in enumerate('abc'):
    print(index, element)
```

```
0 a
1 b
2 c
```

Comparing and Sorting

The relational operators work with tuples and other sequences. For example, if you use the < operator with tuples, it starts by comparing the first element from each sequence. If they are equal, it goes on to the next pair of elements, and so on, until it finds a pair that differ:

```
(0, 1, 2) < (0, 3, 4)
```

```
True
```

Subsequent elements are not considered—even if they are really big:

```
(0, 1, 2000000) < (0, 3, 4)
```

```
True
```

This way of comparing tuples is useful for sorting a list of tuples, or finding the minimum or maximum. As an example, let's find the most common letter in a word. In Chapter 10, we wrote `value_counts`, which takes a string and returns a dictionary that maps from each letter to the number of times it appears:

```
def value_counts(string):
    counter = {}
    for letter in string:
        if letter not in counter:
            counter[letter] = 1
        else:
            counter[letter] += 1
    return counter
```

Here is the result for the string `'banana'`:

```
counter = value_counts('banana')
counter
```

```
{'b': 1, 'a': 3, 'n': 2}
```

With only three items, we can easily see that the most frequent letter is `'a'`, which appears three times. But if there were more items, it would be useful to sort them automatically. We can get the items from `counter` like this:

```
items = counter.items()
items
```

```
dict_items([('b', 1), ('a', 3), ('n', 2)])
```

The result is a `dict_items` object that behaves like a list of tuples, so we can sort it, like this:

```
sorted(items)
```

```
[('a', 3), ('b', 1), ('n', 2)]
```

The default behavior is to use the first element from each tuple to sort the list, and use the second element to break ties.

However, to find the items with the highest counts, we want to use the second element to sort the list. We can do that by writing a function that takes a tuple and returns the second element:

```
def second_element(t):
    return t[1]
```

Then we can pass that function to `sorted` as an optional argument called key, which indicates that this function should be used to compute the **sort key** for each item:

```
sorted_items = sorted(items, key=second_element)
sorted_items
```

```
[('b', 1), ('n', 2), ('a', 3)]
```

The sort key determines the order of the items in the list. The letter with the lowest count appears first, and the letter with the highest count appears last. So we can find the most common letter like this:

```
sorted_items[-1]
```

```
('a', 3)
```

If we only want the maximum, we don't have to sort the list. We can use max, which also takes key as an optional argument:

```
max(items, key=second_element)
```

```
('a', 3)
```

To find the letter with the lowest count, we could use min the same way.

Inverting a Dictionary

Suppose you want to invert a dictionary so you can look up a value and get the corresponding key. For example, if you have a word counter that maps from each word to the number of times it appears, you could make a dictionary that maps from integers to the words that appear that number of times.

But there's a problem—the keys in a dictionary have to be unique, but the values don't. For example, in a word counter, there could be many words with the same count.

So one way to invert a dictionary is to create a new dictionary where the values are lists of keys from the original. As an example, let's count the letters in `parrot`:

```
d = value_counts('parrot')
d
```

```
{'p': 1, 'a': 1, 'r': 2, 'o': 1, 't': 1}
```

If we invert this dictionary, the result should be {1: ['p', 'a', 'o', 't'], 2: ['r']}, which indicates that the letters that appear once are 'p', 'a', 'o', and 't', and the letter that appears twice is 'r'.

The following function takes a dictionary and returns its inverse as a new dictionary:

```
def invert_dict(d):
    new = {}
    for key, value in d.items():
        if value not in new:
            new[value] = [key]
        else:
            new[value].append(key)
    return new
```

The `for` statement loops through the keys and values in d. If the value is not already in the new dictionary, it is added and associated with a list that contains a single element. Otherwise it is appended to the existing list.

We can test it like this:

```
invert_dict(d)
```

```
{1: ['p', 'a', 'o', 't'], 2: ['r']}
```

And we get the result we expected.

This is the first example we've seen where the values in the dictionary are lists. We will see more!

Debugging

Lists, dictionaries, and tuples are **data structures**. In this chapter we are starting to see compound data structures, like lists of tuples, or dictionaries that contain tuples as keys and lists as values. Compound data structures are useful, but they are prone to errors caused when a data structure has the wrong type, size, or structure. For example, if a function expects a list of integers and you give it a plain old integer (not in a list), it probably won't work.

To help debug these kinds of errors, I wrote a module called `structshape` that provides a function, also called `structshape`, that takes any kind of data structure as an argument and returns a string that summarizes its structure. You can download it from *https://raw.githubusercontent.com/AllenDowney/ThinkPython/v3/structshape.py*.

We can import it like this:

```
from structshape import structshape
```

Here's an example with a simple list:

```
t = [1, 2, 3]
structshape(t)
```

```
'list of 3 int'
```

Here's a list of lists:

```
t2 = [[1,2], [3,4], [5,6]]
structshape(t2)
```

```
'list of 3 list of 2 int'
```

If the elements of the list are not the same type, `structshape` groups them by type:

```
t3 = [1, 2, 3, 4.0, '5', '6', [7], [8], 9]
structshape(t3)
```

```
'list of (3 int, float, 2 str, 2 list of int, int)'
```

Here's a list of tuples:

```
s = 'abc'
lt = list(zip(t, s))
structshape(lt)
```

```
'list of 3 tuple of (int, str)'
```

And here's a dictionary with three items that map integers to strings:

```
d = dict(lt)
structshape(d)
```

```
'dict of 3 int->str'
```

If you are having trouble keeping track of your data structures, `structshape` can help.

Glossary

tuple: An immutable object that contains a sequence of values.

pack: Collect multiple arguments into a tuple.

unpack: Treat a tuple (or other sequence) as multiple arguments.

zip object: The result of calling the built-in function `zip`, can be used to loop through a sequence of tuples.

enumerate object: The result of calling the built-in function `enumerate`, can be used to loop through a sequence of tuples.

sort key: A value, or function that computes a value, used to sort the elements of a collection.

data structure: A collection of values, organized to perform certain operations efficiently.

Exercises

Ask a Virtual Assistant

The exercises in this chapter might be more difficult than exercises in previous chapters, so I encourage you to get help from a virtual assistant. When you pose more difficult questions, you might find that the answers are not correct on the first attempt, so this is a chance to practice crafting good prompts and following up with good refinements.

One strategy you might consider is to break a big problem into pieces that can be solved with simple functions. Ask the virtual assistant to write the functions and test them. Then, once they are working, ask for a solution to the original problem.

For some of the following exercises, I make suggestions about which data structures and algorithms to use. You might find these suggestions useful when you work on the problems, but they are also good prompts to pass along to a virtual assistant.

Exercise

In this chapter I said that tuples can be used as keys in dictionaries because they are hashable, and they are hashable because they are immutable. But that is not always true.

If a tuple contains a mutable value, like a list or a dictionary, the tuple is no longer hashable because it contains elements that are not hashable. As an example, here's a tuple that contains two lists of integers:

```
list0 = [1, 2, 3]
list1 = [4, 5]

t = (list0, list1)
t
```

```
([1, 2, 3], [4, 5])
```

Write a line of code that appends the value 6 to the end of the second list in t. If you display t, the result should be ([1, 2, 3], [4, 5, 6]):

```
t[1].append(6)
t
```

```
([1, 2, 3], [4, 5, 6])
```

Try to create a dictionary that maps from t to a string, and confirm that you get a TypeError.

For more on this topic, ask a virtual assistant, "Are Python tuples always hashable?"

Exercise

In this chapter we made a dictionary that maps from each letter to its index in the alphabet:

```
letters = 'abcdefghijklmnopqrstuvwxyz'
numbers = range(len(letters))
letter_map = dict(zip(letters, numbers))
```

For example, the index of 'a' is 0:

```
letter_map['a']
```

```
0
```

To go in the other direction, we can use list indexing. For example, the letter at index 1 is 'b':

```
letters[1]
```

```
'b'
```

We can use letter_map and letters to encode and decode words using a Caesar cipher.

A Caesar cipher is a weak form of encryption that involves shifting each letter by a fixed number of places in the alphabet, wrapping around to the beginning if necessary. For example, 'a' shifted by 2 is 'c', and 'z' shifted by 1 is 'a'.

Write a function called shift_word that takes as parameters a string and an integer, and returns a new string that contains the letters from the string shifted by the given number of places.

To test your function, confirm that "cheer" shifted by 7 is "jolly," and "melon" shifted by 16 is "cubed."

Hint: use the modulus operator to wrap around from 'z' back to 'a'. Loop through the letters of the word, shift each one, and append the result to a list of letters. Then use join to concatenate the letters into a string.

Exercise

Write a function called most_frequent_letters that takes a string and prints the letters in decreasing order of frequency.

To get the items in decreasing order, you can use reversed along with sorted or you can pass reverse=True as a keyword parameter to sorted.

Exercise

In a previous exercise, we tested whether two strings are anagrams by sorting the letters in both words and checking whether the sorted letters are the same. Now let's make the problem a little more challenging.

We'll write a program that takes a list of words and prints all the sets of words that are anagrams. Here is an example of what the output might look like:

```
['deltas', 'desalt', 'lasted', 'salted', 'slated', 'staled']
['retainers', 'ternaries']
['generating', 'greatening']
['resmelts', 'smelters', 'termless']
```

Hint: for each word in the word list, sort the letters and join them back into a string. Make a dictionary that maps from this sorted string to a list of words that are anagrams of it.

Exercise

Write a function called word_distance that takes two words with the same length and returns the number of places where the two words differ.

Hint: use zip to loop through the corresponding letters of the words.

Exercise

"Metathesis" is the transposition of letters in a word. Two words form a "metathesis pair" if you can transform one into the other by swapping two letters, like converse and conserve. Write a program that finds all of the metathesis pairs in the word list.

Hint: the words in a metathesis pair must be anagrams of each other.

Credit: this exercise is inspired by an example at *http://puzzlers.org*.

CHAPTER 12

Text Analysis and Generation

At this point we have covered Python's core data structures—lists, dictionaries, and tuples—and some algorithms that use them. In this chapter, we'll use them to explore text analysis and Markov generation:

- Text analysis is a way to describe the statistical relationships between the words in a document, like the probability that one word is followed by another.
- Markov generation is a way to generate new text with words and phrases similar to the original text.

These algorithms are similar to parts of a large language model (LLM), which is the key component of a chatbot.

We'll start by counting the number of times each word appears in a book. Then we'll look at pairs of words and make a list of the words that can follow each word. We'll make a simple version of a Markov generator, and as an exercise, you'll have a chance to make a more general version.

Unique Words

As a first step toward text analysis, let's read a book—*The Strange Case of Dr. Jekyll and Mr. Hyde* by Robert Louis Stevenson—and count the number of unique words. Instructions for downloading the book are in the notebook for this chapter:

```
filename = 'dr_jekyll.txt'
```

We'll use a for loop to read lines from the file and split to divide the lines into words. Then, to keep track of unique words, we'll store each word as a key in a dictionary:

```
unique_words = {}
    for line in open(filename):
        seq = line.split()
        for word in seq:
            unique_words[word] = 1

len(unique_words)
```

```
6040
```

The length of the dictionary is the number of unique words—about 6000 by this way of counting. But if we inspect them, we'll see that some are not valid words.

For example, let's look at the longest words in unique_words. We can use sorted to sort the words, passing the len function as a keyword argument so the words are sorted by length:

```
sorted(unique_words, key=len)[-5:]
```

```
['chocolate-coloured',
 'superiors—behold!"',
 'coolness—frightened',
 'gentleman—something',
 'pocket-handkerchief.']
```

The slice index, [-5:], selects the last 5 elements of the sorted list, which are the longest words.

The list includes some legitimately long words, like "circumscription," and some hyphenated words, like "chocolate-coloured." But some of the longest "words" are actually two words separated by a dash. And other words include punctuation like periods, exclamation points, and quotation marks.

So, before we move on, let's deal with dashes and other punctuation.

Punctuation

To identify the words in the text, we need to deal with two issues:

- When a dash appears in a line, we should replace it with a space—then when we use split, the words will be separated.

- After splitting the words, we can use strip to remove punctuation.

To handle the first issue, we can use the following function, which takes a string, replaces dashes with spaces, splits the string, and returns the resulting list:

```
def split_line(line):
    return line.replace('-', ' ').split()
```

Notice that `split_line` only replaces dashes, not hyphens.

Here's an example:

```
split_line('coolness-frightened')
```

```
['coolness', 'frightened']
```

Now, to remove punctuation from the beginning and end of each word, we can use `strip`, but we need a list of characters that are considered punctuation.

Characters in Python strings are in Unicode, which is an international standard used to represent letters in nearly every alphabet, numbers, symbols, punctuation marks, and more. The `unicodedata` module provides a `category` function we can use to tell which characters are punctuation. Given a letter, it returns a string with information about what category the letter is in:

```
import unicodedata

unicodedata.category('A')
```

```
'Lu'
```

The category string of `'A'` is `'Lu'`—the `'L'` means it is a letter and the `'u'` means it is uppercase.

The category string of `'.'` is `'Po'`—the `'P'` means it is punctuation, the `'o'` means its subcategory is "other":

```
unicodedata.category('.')
```

```
'Po'
```

We can find the punctuation marks in the book by checking for characters with categories that begin with `'P'`. The following loop stores the unique punctuation marks in a dictionary:

```
punc_marks = {}
for line in open(filename):
    for char in line:
        category = unicodedata.category(char)
        if category.startswith('P'):
            punc_marks[char] = 1
```

To make a list of punctuation marks, we can join the keys of the dictionary into a string:

```
punctuation = ''.join(punc_marks)
print(punctuation)
```

.';,-"":?-'!()_

Now that we know which characters in the book are punctuation, we can write a function that takes a word, strips punctuation from the beginning and end, and converts it to lowercase:

```
def clean_word(word):
    return word.strip(punctuation).lower()
```

Here's an example:

```
clean_word('"Behold!"')
```

```
'behold'
```

Because strip removes characters from the beginning and end, it leaves hyphenated words alone:

```
clean_word('pocket-handkerchief')
```

```
'pocket-handkerchief'
```

Now here's a loop that uses split_line and clean_word to identify the unique words in the book:

```
unique_words2 = {}
for line in open(filename):
    for word in split_line(line):
        word = clean_word(word)
        unique_words2[word] = 1

len(unique_words2)
```

```
4005
```

With this stricter definition of what a word is, there are about four thousand unique words. And we can confirm that the list of longest words has been cleaned up:

```
sorted(unique_words2, key=len)[-5:]
```

```
['circumscription',
 'unimpressionable',
 'fellow-creatures',
 'chocolate-coloured',
 'pocket-handkerchief']
```

Now let's see how many times each word is used.

Word Frequencies

The following loop computes the frequency of each unique word:

```
word_counter = {}
for line in open(filename):
    for word in split_line(line):
        word = clean_word(word)
        if word not in word_counter:
            word_counter[word] = 1
        else:
            word_counter[word] += 1
```

The first time we see a word, we initialize its frequency to 1. If we see the same word again later, we increment its frequency.

To see which words appear most often, we can use items to get the key-value pairs from word_counter, and sort them by the second element of the pair, which is the frequency. First we'll define a function that selects the second element:

```
def second_element(t):
    return t[1]
```

Now we can use sorted with two keyword arguments:

key=second_element
    The items will be sorted according to the frequencies of the words.

reverse=True
    The items will be sorted in reverse order, with the most frequent words first.

```
items = sorted(word_counter.items(), key=second_element, reverse=True)
```

Here are the five most frequent words:

```
for word, freq in items[:5]:
    print(freq, word, sep='\t')
```

```
1614    the
972     and
941     of
640     to
640     i
```

In the next section, we'll encapsulate this loop in a function. And we'll use it to demonstrate a new feature—optional parameters.

Optional Parameters

We've used built-in functions that take optional parameters. For example, round takes an optional parameter called ndigits that indicates how many decimal places to keep:

```
round(3.141592653589793, ndigits=3)
```

```
3.142
```

But it's not just built-in functions—we can write functions with optional parameters, too. For example, the following function takes two parameters, word_counter and num:

```
def print_most_common(word_counter, num=5):
    items = sorted(word_counter.items(), key=second_element, reverse=True)

    for word, freq in items[:num]:
        print(freq, word, sep='\t')
```

The second parameter looks like an assignment statement, but it's not—it's an optional parameter.

If you call this function with one argument, num gets the **default value**, which is 5:

```
print_most_common(word_counter)
```

```
1614    the
972     and
941     of
640     to
640     i
```

If you call this function with two arguments, the second argument gets assigned to num instead of the default value:

```
print_most_common(word_counter, 3)
```

```
1614    the
972     and
941     of
```

In that case, we would say the optional argument **overrides** the default value.

If a function has both required and optional parameters, all of the required parameters have to come first, followed by the optional ones.

Dictionary Subtraction

Suppose we want to spellcheck a book—that is, find a list of words that might be misspelled. One way to do that is to find words in the book that don't appear in a list of valid words. In previous chapters, we've used a list of words that are considered valid in word games like Scrabble. Now we'll use this list to spellcheck Robert Louis Stevenson's work.

We can think of this problem as set subtraction—that is, we want to find all the words from one set (the words in the book) that are not in the other (the words in the list).

As we've done before, we can read the contents of *words.txt* and split it into a list of strings:

```
word_list = open('words.txt').read().split()
```

Then we'll store the words as keys in a dictionary so we can use the in operator to check quickly whether a word is valid:

```
valid_words = {}
for word in word_list:
    valid_words[word] = 1
```

Now, to identify words that appear in the book but not in the word list, we'll use subtract, which takes two dictionaries as parameters and returns a new dictionary that contains all the keys from one that are not in the other:

```
def subtract(d1, d2):
    res = {}
    for key in d1:
        if key not in d2:
            res[key] = d1[key]
    return res
```

Here's how we use it:

```
diff = subtract(word_counter, valid_words)
```

To get a sample of words that might be misspelled, we can print the most common words in `diff`:

```
print_most_common(diff)
```

```
640    i
628    a
128    utterson
124    mr
98     hyde
```

The most common "misspelled" words are mostly names and a few single-letter words (Mr. Utterson is Dr. Jekyll's friend and lawyer).

If we select words that only appear once, they are more likely to be actual misspellings. We can do that by looping through the items and making a list of words with a frequency of 1:

```
singletons = []
for word, freq in diff.items():
    if freq == 1:
        singletons.append(word)
```

Here are the last few elements of the list:

```
singletons[-5:]
```

```
['gesticulated', 'abjection', 'circumscription', 'reindue', 'fearstruck']
```

Most of them are valid words that are not in the word list. But `'reindue'` appears to be a misspelling of `'reinduce'`, so at least we found one legitimate error.

Random Numbers

As a step toward Markov text generation, next we'll choose a random sequence of words from `word_counter`. But first let's talk about randomness.

Given the same inputs, most computer programs are **deterministic**, which means they generate the same outputs every time. Determinism is usually a good thing, since we expect the same calculation to yield the same result. For some applications though, we want the computer to be unpredictable. Games are one example, but there are more.

Making a program truly nondeterministic turns out to be difficult, but there are ways to fake it. One is to use algorithms that generate **pseudorandom** numbers. Pseudorandom numbers are not truly random because they are generated by a deterministic computation, but just by looking at the numbers it is all but impossible to distinguish them from random.

The random module provides functions that generate pseudorandom numbers—which I will simply call "random" from here on. We can import it like this:

```
import random
```

The random module provides a function called choice that chooses an element from a list at random, with every element having the same probability of being chosen:

```
t = [1, 2, 3]
random.choice(t)
```

```
1
```

If you call the function again, you might get the same element again, or a different one:

```
random.choice(t)
```

```
2
```

In the long run, we expect to get every element about the same number of times.

If you use choice with a dictionary, you get a KeyError:

```
random.choice(word_counter)
```

```
KeyError: 422
```

To choose a random key, you have to put the keys in a list and then call choice:

```
words = list(word_counter)
random.choice(words)
```

```
'posture'
```

If we generate a random sequence of words, it doesn't make much sense:

```
for i in range(6):
    word = random.choice(words)
    print(word, end=' ')
```

```
ill-contained written apocryphal nor busy spoke
```

Part of the problem is that we are not taking into account that some words are more common than others. The results will be better if we choose words with different "weights," so that some are chosen more often than others.

If we use the values from word_counter as weights, each word is chosen with a probability that depends on its frequency:

```
weights = word_counter.values()
```

The random module provides another function called choices that takes weights as an optional argument:

```
random.choices(words, weights=weights)
```

```
['than']
```

And it takes another optional argument, k, that specifies the number of words to select:

```
random_words = random.choices(words, weights=weights, k=6)
random_words
```

```
['reach', 'streets', 'edward', 'a', 'said', 'to']
```

The result is a list of strings that we can join into something that looks more like a sentence:

```
' '.join(random_words)
```

```
'reach streets edward a said to'
```

If you choose words from the book at random, you get a sense of the vocabulary, but a series of random words seldom makes sense because there is no relationship between successive words. For example, in a real sentence you expect an article like "the" to be followed by an adjective or a noun, and probably not a verb or adverb. So the next step is to look at these relationships between words.

Bigrams

Instead of looking at one word at a time, now we'll look at sequences of two words, which are called **bigrams**. A sequence of three words is called a **trigram**, and a sequence with some unspecified number of words is called an **n-gram**.

Let's write a program that finds all of the bigrams in the book and the number of times each one appears. To store the results, we'll use a dictionary where:

- The keys are tuples of strings that represent bigrams, and
- The values are integers that represent frequencies.

Let's call it `bigram_counter`:

```
bigram_counter = {}
```

The following function takes a list of two strings as a parameter. First it makes a tuple of the two strings, which can be used as a key in a dictionary. Then it adds the key to `bigram_counter`, if it doesn't exist, or increments the frequency if it does:

```
def count_bigram(bigram):
    key = tuple(bigram)
    if key not in bigram_counter:
        bigram_counter[key] = 1
    else:
        bigram_counter[key] += 1
```

As we go through the book, we have to keep track of each pair of consecutive words. So if we see the sequence "man is not truly one," we would add the bigrams "man is," "is not," "not truly," and so on.

To keep track of these bigrams, we'll use a list called `window`, because it is like a window that slides over the pages of the book, showing only two words at a time. Initially, `window` is empty:

```
window = []
```

We'll use the following function to process the words one at a time:

```
def process_word(word):
    window.append(word)

    if len(window) == 2:
        count_bigram(window)
        window.pop(0)
```

The first time this function is called, it appends the given word to `window`. Since there is only one word in the window, we don't have a bigram yet, so the function ends.

The second time it's called—and every time thereafter—it appends a second word to `window`. Since there are two words in the window, it calls `count_bigram` to keep track of how many times each bigram appears. Then it uses `pop` to remove the first word from the window.

The following program loops through the words in the book and processes them one at a time:

```
for line in open(filename):
    for word in split_line(line):
        word = clean_word(word)
        process_word(word)
```

The result is a dictionary that maps from each bigram to the number of times it appears. We can use `print_most_common` to see the most common bigrams:

```
print_most_common(bigram_counter)
```

```
178    ('of', 'the')
139    ('in', 'the')
94     ('it', 'was')
80     ('and', 'the')
73     ('to', 'the')
```

Looking at these results, we can get a sense of which pairs of words are most likely to appear together. We can also use the results to generate random text, like this:

```
bigrams = list(bigram_counter)
weights = bigram_counter.values()
random_bigrams = random.choices(bigrams, weights=weights, k=6)
```

`bigrams` is a list of the bigrams that appear in the book. `weights` is a list of their frequencies, so `random_bigrams` is a sample where the probability a bigram is selected is proportional to its frequency.

Here are the results:

```
for pair in random_bigrams:
    print(' '.join(pair), end=' ')
```

```
to suggest this preface to detain fact is above all the laboratory
```

This way of generating text is better than choosing random words, but still doesn't make a lot of sense.

Markov Analysis

We can do better with Markov chain text analysis, which computes, for each word in a text, the list of words that come next. As an example, we'll analyze these lyrics from the Monty Python song "Eric, the Half a Bee":

```
song = """
Half a bee, philosophically,
Must, ipso facto, half not be.
But half the bee has got to be
Vis a vis, its entity. D'you see?
"""
```

To store the results, we'll use a dictionary that maps from each word to the list of words that follow it:

```
successor_map = {}
```

As an example, let's start with the first two words of the song:

```
first = 'half'
second = 'a'
```

If the first word is not in `successor_map`, we have to add a new item that maps from the first word to a list containing the second word:

```
successor_map[first] = [second]
successor_map
```

```
{'half': ['a']}
```

If the first word is already in the dictionary, we can look it up to get the list of successors we've seen so far, and append the new one:

```
first = 'half'
second = 'not'

successor_map[first].append(second)
successor_map
```

```
{'half': ['a', 'not']}
```

The following function encapsulates these steps:

```
def add_bigram(bigram):
    first, second = bigram

    if first not in successor_map:
        successor_map[first] = [second]
```

```
    else:
        successor_map[first].append(second)
```

If the same bigram appears more that once, the second word is added to the list more than once. In this way, `successor_map` keeps track of how many times each successor appears.

As we did in the previous section, we'll use a list called `window` to store pairs of consecutive words. And we'll use the following function to process the words one at a time:

```
def process_word_bigram(word):
    window.append(word)

    if len(window) == 2:
        add_bigram(window)
        window.pop(0)
```

Here's how we use it to process the words in the song:

```
successor_map = {}
window = []

for word in song.split():
    word = clean_word(word)
    process_word_bigram(word)
```

And here are the results:

```
successor_map
```

```
{'half': ['a', 'not', 'the'],
 'a': ['bee', 'vis'],
 'bee': ['philosophically', 'has'],
 'philosophically': ['must'],
 'must': ['ipso'],
 'ipso': ['facto'],
 'facto': ['half'],
 'not': ['be'],
 'be': ['but', 'vis'],
 'but': ['half'],
 'the': ['bee'],
 'has': ['got'],
 'got': ['to'],
 'to': ['be'],
 'vis': ['a', 'its'],
 'its': ['entity'],
 'entity': ["d'you"],
 "d'you": ['see']}
```

The word 'half' can be followed by 'a', 'not', or 'the'. The word 'a' can be followed by 'bee' or 'vis'. Most of the other words appear only once, so they are followed by only a single word.

Now let's analyze the book:

```
successor_map = {}
window = []

for line in open(filename):
    for word in split_line(line):
        word = clean_word(word)
        process_word_bigram(word)
```

We can look up any word and find the words that can follow it:

```
successor_map['going']
```

```
['east', 'in', 'to', 'to', 'up', 'to', 'of']
```

In this list of successors, notice that the word 'to' appears three times—the other successors only appear once.

Generating Text

We can use the results from the previous section to generate new text with the same relationships between consecutive words as in the original. Here's how it works:

- Starting with any word that appears in the text, we look up its possible successors and choose one at random.
- Then, using the chosen word, we look up its possible successors and choose one at random.

We can repeat this process to generate as many words as we want. As an example, let's start with the word 'although'. Here are the words that can follow it:

```
word = 'although'
successors = successor_map[word]
successors
```

```
['i', 'a', 'it', 'the', 'we', 'they', 'i']
```

We can use `choice` to choose from the list with equal probability:

```
word = random.choice(successors)
word
```

```
'i'
```

If the same word appears more than once in the list, it is more likely to be selected.

Repeating these steps, we can use the following loop to generate a longer series:

```
for i in range(10):
    successors = successor_map[word]
    word = random.choice(successors)
    print(word, end=' ')
```

```
continue to hesitate and swallowed the smile withered from that
```

The result sounds more like a real sentence, but it still doesn't make much sense.

We can do better using more than one word as a key in `successor_map`. For example, we can make a dictionary that maps from each bigram—or trigram—to the list of words that come next. As an exercise, you'll have a chance to implement this analysis and see what the results look like.

Debugging

At this point we are writing more substantial programs, and you might find that you are spending more time debugging. If you are stuck on a difficult bug, here are a few things to try:

Reading
> Examine your code, read it back to yourself, and check that it says what you meant to say.

Running
> Experiment by making changes and running different versions. Often, if you display the right thing at the right place in the program, the problem becomes obvious, but sometimes you have to build scaffolding.

Ruminating
> Take some time to think! What kind of error is it: syntax, runtime, or semantic? What information can you get from the error messages or from the output of the program? What kind of error could cause the problem you're seeing? What did you change last, before the problem appeared?

Rubberducking

If you explain the problem to someone else, you sometimes find the answer before you finish asking the question. Often you don't need the other person; you could just talk to a rubber duck. And that's the origin of the well-known strategy called **rubber duck debugging**. I am not making this up (*https://en.wikipedia.org/wiki/Rubber_duck_debugging*).

Retreating

At some point, the best thing to do is back up—undoing recent changes—until you get to a program that works. Then you can start rebuilding.

Resting

If you give your brain a break, sometimes it will find the problem for you.

Beginning programmers sometimes get stuck on one of these activities and forget the others. Each activity comes with its own failure mode.

For example, reading your code works if the problem is a typographical error, but not if the problem is a conceptual misunderstanding. If you don't understand what your program does, you can read it a hundred times and never see the error, because the error is in your head.

Running experiments can work, especially if you run small, simple tests. But if you run experiments without thinking or reading your code, it can take a long time to figure out what's happening.

You have to take time to think. Debugging is like an experimental science. You should have at least one hypothesis about what the problem is. If there are two or more possibilities, try to think of a test that would eliminate one of them.

But even the best debugging techniques will fail if there are too many errors, or if the code you are trying to fix is too big and complicated. Sometimes the best option is to retreat, simplifying the program until you get back to something that works.

Beginning programmers are often reluctant to retreat because they can't stand to delete a line of code (even if it's wrong). If it makes you feel better, copy your program into another file before you start stripping it down. Then you can copy the pieces back one at a time.

Finding a hard bug requires reading, running, ruminating, retreating, and sometimes resting. If you get stuck on one of these activities, try the others.

Glossary

default value: The value assigned to a parameter if no argument is provided.

override: To replace a default value with an argument.

deterministic: A deterministic program does the same thing each time it runs, given the same inputs.

pseudorandom: A pseudorandom sequence of numbers appears to be random, but is generated by a deterministic program.

bigram: A sequence of two elements, often words.

trigram: A sequence of three elements.

n-gram: A sequence of an unspecified number of elements.

rubber duck debugging: A way of debugging by explaining a problem aloud to an inanimate object.

Exercises

Ask a Virtual Assistant

In `add_bigram`, the `if` statement creates a new list or appends an element to an existing list, depending on whether the key is already in the dictionary:

```
def add_bigram(bigram):
    first, second = bigram

    if first not in successor_map:
        successor_map[first] = [second]
    else:
        successor_map[first].append(second)
```

Dictionaries provide a method called `setdefault` that we can use to do the same thing more concisely. Ask a virtual assistant how it works, or copy `add_word` into a virtual assistant and ask "Can you rewrite this using `setdefault`?"

In this chapter we implemented Markov chain text analysis and generation. If you are curious, you can ask a virtual assistant for more information on the topic. One of the things you might learn is that virtual assistants use algorithms that are similar in many ways—but also different in important ways. Ask a virtual assistant, "What are the differences between large language models like ChatGPT and Markov chain text analysis?"

Exercise

Write a function that counts the number of times each trigram (sequence of three words) appears. If you test your function with the text of *Dr. Jekyll and Mr. Hyde*, you should find that the most common trigram is "said the lawyer."

Hint: write a function called `count_trigram` that is similar to `count_bigram`. Then write a function called `process_word_trigram` that is similar to `process_word_bigram`.

Exercise

Now let's implement Markov chain text analysis with a mapping from each bigram to a list of possible successors. Starting with `add_bigram`, write a function called `add_trigram` that takes a list of three words and either adds or updates an item in `successor_map`, using the first two words as the key and the third word as a possible successor.

Here's a version of `process_word_trigram` that calls `add_trigram`:

```
def process_word_trigram(word):
    window.append(word)

    if len(window) == 3:
        add_trigram(window)
        window.pop(0)
```

You can use the following loop to test your function with the words from the book:

```
successor_map = {}
window = []

for line in open(filename):
    for word in split_line(line):
        word = clean_word(word)
        process_word_trigram(word)
```

In the next exercise, you'll use the results to generate new random text.

Exercise

For this exercise, we'll assume that `successor_map` is a dictionary that maps from each bigram to the list of words that follow it. To generate random text, we'll start by choosing a random key from `successor_map`:

```
successors = list(successor_map)
bigram = random.choice(successors)
bigram
```

```
('doubted', 'if')
```

Now write a loop that generates 50 more words by following these steps:

1. In `successor_map`, look up the list of words that can follow `bigram`.
2. Choose one of them at random and print it.
3. For the next iteration, make a new bigram that contains the second word from `bigram` and the chosen successor.

For example, if we start with the bigram `('doubted', 'if')` and choose `'from'` as its successor, the next bigram is `('if', 'from')`.

If everything is working, you should find that the generated text is recognizably similar in style to the original, and some phrases make sense, but the text might wander from one topic to another.

As a bonus exercise, modify your solution to the last two exercises to use trigrams as keys in `successor_map`, and see what effect it has on the results.

CHAPTER 13

Files and Databases

Most of the programs we have seen so far are **ephemeral** in the sense that they run for a short time and produce output, but when they end, their data disappears. Each time you run an ephemeral program, it starts with a clean slate.

Other programs are **persistent**: they run for a long time (or all the time); they keep at least some of their data in long-term storage; and if they shut down and restart, they pick up where they left off.

A simple way for programs to maintain their data is by reading and writing text files. A more versatile alternative is to store data in a database. Databases are specialized files that can be read and written more efficiently than text files, and they provide additional capabilities.

In this chapter, we'll write programs that read and write text files and databases, and as an exercise you'll write a program that searches a collection of photos for duplicates. But before you can work with a file, you have to find it, so we'll start with filenames, paths, and directories.

Filenames and Paths

Files are organized into **directories**, also called "folders." Every running program has a **current working directory**, which is the default directory for most operations. For example, when you open a file, Python looks for it in the current working directory.

The os module provides functions for working with files and directories ("os" stands for "operating system"). It provides a function called getcwd that gets the name of the current working directory:

```
import os
os.getcwd()
```

```
'/home/dinsdale'
```

The result in this example is the home directory of a user named dinsdale. A string like '/home/dinsdale' that identifies a file or directory is called a **path**.

A simple filename like 'memo.txt' is also considered a path, but it is a **relative path** because it specifies a filename relative to the current directory. In this example, the current directory is */home/dinsdale*, so 'memo.txt' is equivalent to the complete path '/home/dinsdale/memo.txt'.

A path that begins with / does not depend on the current directory—it is called an **absolute path**. To find the absolute path to a file, you can use abspath:

```
os.path.abspath('memo.txt')
```

```
'/home/dinsdale/memo.txt'
```

The os module provides other functions for working with filenames and paths. list dir returns a list of the contents of the given directory, including files and other directories. Here's an example that lists the contents of a directory named *photos*:

```
os.listdir('photos')
```

```
['notes.txt', 'mar-2023', 'jan-2023', 'feb-2023']
```

This directory contains a text file named *notes.txt* and three directories. The directories contain image files in the JPEG format:

```
os.listdir('photos/jan-2023')
```

```
['photo3.jpg', 'photo2.jpg', 'photo1.jpg']
```

To check whether a file or directory exists, we can use os.path.exists:

```
os.path.exists('photos')
```

```
True
```

```
os.path.exists('photos/apr-2023')
```

```
False
```

To check whether a path refers to a file or directory, we can use `isdir`, which returns `True` if a path refers to a directory:

```
os.path.isdir('photos')
```

```
True
```

And `isfile`, which returns `True` if a path refers to a file:

```
os.path.isfile('photos/notes.txt')
```

```
True
```

One challenge of working with paths is that they look different on different operating systems. On macOS and Unix systems like Linux, the directory and filenames in a path are separated by a forward slash, /. Windows uses a backward slash, \. So, if you you run these examples on Windows, you will see backward slashes in the paths, and you'll have to replace the forward slashes in the examples.

Or, to write code that works on both systems, you can use `os.path.join`, which joins directory and filenames into a path using a forward or backward slash, depending on which operating system you are using:

```
os.path.join('photos', 'jan-2023', 'photo1.jpg')
```

```
'photos/jan-2023/photo1.jpg'
```

Later in this chapter we'll use these functions to search a set of directories and find all of the image files.

f-strings

One way for programs to store data is to write it to a text file. For example, suppose you are a camel spotter, and you want to record the number of camels you have seen during a period of observation. And suppose that in one and a half years, you have spotted 23 camels. The data in your camel-spotting book might look like this:

```
num_years = 1.5
num_camels = 23
```

To write this data to a file, you can use the `write` method, which we saw in "Writing Files" on page 110. The argument of `write` has to be a string, so if we want to put other values in a file, we have to convert them to strings. The easiest way to do that is with the built-in function `str`.

Here's what that looks like:

```
writer = open('camel-spotting-book.txt', 'w')
writer.write(str(num_years))
writer.write(str(num_camels))
writer.close()
```

That works, but `write` doesn't add a space or newline unless you include it explicitly. If we read back the file, we see that the two numbers are run together:

```
open('camel-spotting-book.txt').read()
```

```
'1.523'
```

At the very least, we should add whitespace between the numbers. And while we're at it, let's add some explanatory text.

To write a combination of strings and other values, we can use an **f-string**, which is a string that has the letter `f` before the opening quotation mark, and contains one or more Python expressions in curly braces. The following f-string contains one expression, which is a variable name:

```
f'I have spotted {num_camels} camels'
```

```
'I have spotted 23 camels'
```

The result is a string where the expression has been evaluated and replaced with the result. There can be more than one expression:

```
f'In {num_years} years I have spotted {num_camels} camels'
```

```
'In 1.5 years I have spotted 23 camels'
```

And the expressions can contain operators and function calls:

```
line = f'In {round(num_years * 12)} months I have spotted {num_camels} camels'
line
```

```
'In 18 months I have spotted 23 camels'
```

So we could write the data to a text file like this:

```
writer = open('camel-spotting-book.txt', 'w')
writer.write(f'Years of observation: {num_years}\n')
writer.write(f'Camels spotted: {num_camels}\n')
writer.close()
```

Both f-strings end with the sequence \n, which adds a newline character.

We can read the file back like this:

```
data = open('camel-spotting-book.txt').read()
print(data)
```

```
Years of observation: 1.5
Camels spotted: 23
```

In an f-string, an expression in curly braces is converted to a string, so you can include lists, dictionaries, and other types:

```
t = [1, 2, 3]
d = {'one': 1}
f'Here is a list {t} and a dictionary {d}'
```

```
"Here is a list [1, 2, 3] and a dictionary {'one': 1}"
```

YAML

One of the reasons programs read and write files is to store **configuration data**, which is information that specifies what the program should do, and how.

For example, in a program that searches for duplicate photos, we might have a dictionary called `config` that contains the name of the directory to search, the name of another directory where it should store the results, and a list of file extensions it should use to identify image files.

Here's what it might look like:

```
config = {
    'photo_dir': 'photos',
    'data_dir': 'photo_info',
    'extensions': ['jpg', 'jpeg'],
}
```

To write this data in a text file, we could use f-strings, as in the previous section. But it is easier to use a module called `yaml` that is designed for just this sort of thing.

The `yaml` module provides functions to work with YAML files, which are text files formatted to be easy for humans *and* programs to read and write.

Here's an example that uses the `dump` function to write the `config` dictionary to a YAML file:

```
import yaml

config_filename = 'config.yaml'
writer = open(config_filename, 'w')
yaml.dump(config, writer)
writer.close()
```

If we read back the contents of the file, we can see what the YAML format looks like:

```
readback = open(config_filename).read()
print(readback)
```

```
data_dir: photo_info
extensions:
- jpg
- jpeg
photo_dir: photos
```

Now, we can use `safe_load` to read back the YAML file:

```
reader = open(config_filename)
config_readback = yaml.safe_load(reader)
config_readback
```

```
{'data_dir': 'photo_info',
 'extensions': ['jpg', 'jpeg'],
 'photo_dir': 'photos'}
```

The result is new dictionary that contains the same information as the original, but it is not the same dictionary:

```
config is config_readback
```

```
False
```

Converting an object like a dictionary to a string is called **serialization**. Converting the string back to an object is called **deserialization**. If you serialize and then deserialize an object, the result should be equivalent to the original.

Shelve

So far we've been reading and writing text files—now let's consider databases. A **database** is a file that is organized for storing data. Some databases are organized like a table with rows and columns of information. Others are organized like a dictionary that maps from keys to values; they are sometimes called **key-value stores**.

The `shelve` module provides functions for creating and updating a key-value store called a "shelf." As an example, we'll create a shelf to contain captions for the figures in the *photos* directory. We'll use the `config` dictionary to get the name of the directory where we should put the shelf:

```
config['data_dir']
```

```
'photo_info'
```

We can use `os.makedirs` to create this directory, if it doesn't already exist:

```
os.makedirs(config['data_dir'], exist_ok=True)
```

And use `os.path.join` to make a path that includes the name of the directory and the name of the shelf file, *captions*:

```
db_file = os.path.join(config['data_dir'], 'captions')
db_file
```

```
'photo_info/captions'
```

Now we can use `shelve.open` to open the shelf file. The argument `c` indicates that the file should be created, if necessary:

```
import shelve

db = shelve.open(db_file, 'c')
db
```

```
<shelve.DbfilenameShelf at 0x7f5a2021c310>
```

The return value is officially a `DbfilenameShelf` object, more casually called a shelf object.

The shelf object behaves in many ways like a dictionary. For example, we can use the bracket operator to add an item, which is a mapping from a key to a value:

```
key = 'jan-2023/photo1.jpg'
db[key] = 'Cat nose'
```

In this example, the key is the path to an image file and the value is a string that describes the image.

We also use the bracket operator to look up a key and get the corresponding value:

```
value = db[key]
value
```

```
'Cat nose'
```

If you make another assignment to an existing key, dbm replaces the old value:

```
db[key] = 'Close up view of a cat nose'
db[key]
```

```
'Close up view of a cat nose'
```

Some dictionary methods, like keys, values, and items, also work with database objects:

```
list(db.keys())
```

```
['jan-2023/photo1.jpg']
```

```
list(db.values())
```

```
['Close up view of a cat nose']
```

We can use the in operator to check whether a key appears in the shelf:

```
key in db
```

```
True
```

And we can use a for statement to loop through the keys:

```
for key in db:
    print(key, ':', db[key])
```

```
jan-2023/photo1.jpg : Close up view of a cat nose
```

As with other files, you should close the database when you are done:

```
db.close()
```

Now if we list the contents of the data directory, we see two files:

```
os.listdir(config['data_dir'])
```

```
['captions.dir', 'captions.dat']
```

captions.dat contains the data we just stored. *captions.dir* contains information about the organization of the database that makes it more efficient to access. The suffix *dir* stands for "directory," but it has nothing to do with the directories we've been working with that contain files.

Storing Data Structures

In the previous example, the keys and values in the shelf are strings. But we can also use a shelf to contain data structures like lists and dictionaries.

As an example, let's revisit the anagram example from the "Exercise" on page 169. Recall that we made a dictionary that maps from a sorted string of letters to the list of words that can be spelled with those letters. For example, the key 'opst' maps to the list ['opts', 'post', 'pots', 'spot', 'stop', 'tops'].

We'll use the following function to sort the letters in a word:

```
def sort_word(word):
    return ''.join(sorted(word))
```

And here's an example:

```
word = 'pots'
key = sort_word(word)
key
```

```
'opst'
```

Now let's open a shelf called `anagram_map`. The argument 'n' means we should always create a new, empty shelf, even if one already exists:

```
db = shelve.open('anagram_map', 'n')
```

Now we can add an item to the shelf like this:

```
db[key] = [word]
db[key]
```

```
['pots']
```

In this item, the key is a string and the value is a list of strings.

Now suppose we find another word that contains the same letters, like `tops`:

```
word = 'tops'
key = sort_word(word)
key
```

```
'opst'
```

The key is the same as in the previous example, so we want to append a second word to the same list of strings. Here's how we would do it if db were a dictionary:

```
db[key].append(word)          # INCORRECT
```

But if we run that and then look up the key in the shelf, it looks like it has not been updated:

```
db[key]
```

```
['pots']
```

Here's the problem: when we look up the key, we get a list of strings, but if we modify the list of strings, it does not affect the shelf. If we want to update the shelf, we have to read the old value, update it, and then write the new value back to the shelf:

```
anagram_list = db[key]
anagram_list.append(word)
db[key] = anagram_list
```

Now the value in the shelf is updated:

```
db[key]
```

```
['pots', 'tops']
```

As an exercise, you can finish this example by reading the word list and storing all of the anagrams in a shelf.

Checking for Equivalent Files

Now let's get back to the goal of this chapter: searching for different files that contain the same data. One way to check is to read the contents of both files and compare.

If the files contain images, we have to open them with mode `'rb'`, where `'r'` means we want to read the contents and `'b'` indicates **binary mode**. In binary mode, the contents are not interpreted as text—they are treated as a sequence of bytes.

Here's an example that opens and reads an image file:

```
path1 = 'photos/jan-2023/photo1.jpg'
data1 = open(path1, 'rb').read()
type(data1)
```

```
bytes
```

The result from `read` is a `bytes` object—as the name suggests, it contains a sequence of bytes.

In general, the contents of an image file are not human readable. But if we read the contents from a second file, we can use the == operator to compare:

```
path2 = 'photos/jan-2023/photo2.jpg'
data2 = open(path2, 'rb').read()
data1 == data2
```

```
False
```

These two files are not equivalent.

Let's encapsulate what we have so far in a function:

```
def same_contents(path1, path2):
    data1 = open(path1, 'rb').read()
    data2 = open(path2, 'rb').read()
    return data1 == data2
```

If we have only two files, this function is a good option. But suppose we have a large number of files and we want to know whether any two of them contain the same data. It would be inefficient to compare every pair of files.

An alternative is to use a **hash function**, which takes the contents of a file and computes a **digest**, which is usually a large integer. If two files contain the same data, they will have the same digest. If two files differ, they will *almost always* have different digests.

The `hashlib` module provides several hash functions—the one we'll use is called `md5`. We'll start by using `hashlib.md5` to create a HASH object:

```
import hashlib

md5_hash = hashlib.md5()
type(md5_hash)
```

```
_hashlib.HASH
```

The `HASH` object provides an `update` function that takes the contents of the file as an argument:

```
md5_hash.update(data1)
```

Now we can use `hexdigest` to get the digest as a string of hexadecimal digits that represent an integer in base 16:

```
digest = md5_hash.hexdigest()
digest
```

```
'aa1d2fc25b7ae247b2931f5a0882fa37'
```

The following function encapsulates these steps:

```
def md5_digest(filename):
    data = open(filename, 'rb').read()
    md5_hash = hashlib.md5()
    md5_hash.update(data)
    digest = md5_hash.hexdigest()
    return digest
```

If we hash the contents of a different file, we can confirm that we get a different digest:

```
filename2 = 'photos/feb-2023/photo2.jpg'
md5_digest(filename2)
```

```
'6a501b11b01f89af9c3f6591d7f02c49'
```

Now we have almost everything we need to find equivalent files. The last step is to search a directory and find all of the image files.

Walking Directories

The following function takes as an argument the directory we want to search. It uses `listdir` to loop through the contents of the directory. When it finds a file, it prints its complete path. When it finds a directory, it calls itself recursively to search the subdirectory:

```
def walk(dirname):
    for name in os.listdir(dirname):
        path = os.path.join(dirname, name)

        if os.path.isfile(path):
            print(path)
        elif os.path.isdir(path):
            walk(path)
```

We can use it like this:

```
walk('photos')
```

```
photos/notes.txt
photos/mar-2023/photo2.jpg
photos/mar-2023/photo1.jpg
photos/jan-2023/photo3.jpg
photos/jan-2023/photo2.jpg
photos/jan-2023/photo1.jpg
photos/feb-2023/photo2.jpg
photos/feb-2023/photo1.jpg
```

The order of the results depends on details of the operating system.

Here is a more general version of `walk` that takes as a second parameter a function object. Instead of printing the path of the files it discovers, it calls this function and passes the path as a parameter:

```
def walk(dirname, visit_func):
    for name in os.listdir(dirname):
        path = os.path.join(dirname, name)

        if os.path.isfile(path):
            visit_func(path)
        else:
            walk(path, visit_func)
```

Here's an example where we pass `print` as an argument, so when `walk` calls `visit_func`, it prints the paths of the files it discovers:

```
walk('photos', print)
```

```
photos/notes.txt
photos/mar-2023/photo2.jpg
photos/mar-2023/photo1.jpg
photos/jan-2023/photo3.jpg
photos/jan-2023/photo2.jpg
photos/jan-2023/photo1.jpg
photos/feb-2023/photo2.jpg
photos/feb-2023/photo1.jpg
```

The parameter is called `visit_func` because it suggests that as we "walk" around the directory, we "visit" each file.

Debugging

When you are reading and writing files, you might run into problems with whitespace. These errors can be hard to debug because spaces, tabs, and newlines are normally invisible:

```
s = '1 2\t 3\n 4'
print(s)
```

```
1 2	 3
 4
```

The built-in function `repr` can help. It takes any object as an argument and returns a string representation of the object. For strings, it represents whitespace characters with backslash sequences:

```
print(repr(s))
```

```
'1 2\t 3\n 4'
```

This can be helpful for debugging.

One other problem you might run into is that different systems use different characters to indicate the end of a line. Some systems use a newline, represented as \n. Others use a return character, represented as \r. Some use both. If you move files between different systems, these inconsistencies can cause problems.

Filename capitalization is another issue you might encounter if you work with different operating systems. In macOS and Unix, filenames can contain lowercase and uppercase letters, digits, and most symbols. But many Windows applications ignore the difference between lowercase and uppercase letters, and several symbols that are allowed in macOS and Unix are not allowed in Windows.

Glossary

ephemeral: An ephemeral program typically runs for a short time and, when it ends, its data is lost.

persistent: A persistent program runs indefinitely and keeps at least some of its data in permanent storage.

directory: A collection of files and other directories.

current working directory: The default directory used by a program unless another directory is specified.

path: A string that specifies a sequence of directories, often leading to a file.

relative path: A path that starts from the current working directory, or some other specified directory.

absolute path: A path that does not depend on the current directory.

f-string: A string that has the letter f before the opening quotation mark, and contains one or more expressions in curly braces.

configuration data: Data, often stored in a file, that specifies what a program should do and how.

serialization: Converting an object to a string.

deserialization: Converting a string to an object.

database: A file whose contents are organized to perform certain operations efficiently.

key-value stores: A database whose contents are organized like a dictionary with keys that correspond to values.

binary mode: A way of writing a file so the contents are interpreted as sequence of bytes rather than a sequence of characters.

hash function: A function that takes an object and computes an integer, which is sometimes called a digest.

digest: The result of a hash function, especially when it is used to check whether two objects are the same.

Exercises

Ask a Virtual Assistant

There are several topics that came up in this chapter that I did not explain in detail. Here are some questions you can ask a virtual assistant to get more information:

- "What are the differences between ephemeral and persistent programs?"
- "What are some examples of persistent programs?"
- "What's the difference between a relative path and an absolute path?"
- "Why does the yaml module have functions called load and safe_load?"
- "When I write a Python shelf, what are the files with suffixes dat and dir?"
- "Other than key-values stores, what other kinds of databases are there?"
- "When I read a file, what's the difference between binary mode and text mode?"
- "What are the differences between a bytes object and a string?"
- "What is a hash function?"
- "What is an MD5 digest?"

As always, if you get stuck on any of the following exercises, consider asking a virtual assistant for help. Along with your question, you might want to paste in the relevant functions from this chapter.

Exercise

Write a function called replace_all that takes as arguments a pattern string, a replacement string, and two filenames. It should read the first file and write the contents into the second file (creating it, if necessary). If the pattern string appears anywhere in the contents, it should be replaced with the replacement string.

To test your function, read the file *photos/notes.txt*, replace 'photos' with 'images', and write the result to the file *photos/new_notes.txt*.

Exercise

In "Storing Data Structures" on page 199, we used the shelve module to make a key-value store that maps from a sorted string of letters to a list of anagrams. To finish the example, write a function called add_word that takes as arguments a string and a shelf object.

It should sort the letters of the word to make a key, then check whether the key is already in the shelf. If not, it should make a list that contains the new word and add it to the shelf. If the key is already in the shelf, it should append the new word to the existing value.

Exercise

In a large collection of files, there may be more than one copy of the same file, stored in different directories or with different filenames. The goal of this exercise is to search for duplicates. As an example, we'll work with image files in the *photos* directory.

Here's how it will work:

- We'll use the walk function from "Walking Directories" on page 203 to search this directory for files that end with one of the extensions in config ['extensions'].

- For each file, we'll use md5_digest from "Checking for Equivalent Files" on page 201 to compute a digest of the contents.

- Using a shelf, we'll make a mapping from each digest to a list of paths with that digest.

- Finally, we'll search the shelf for any digests that map to multiple files.

- If we find any, we'll use same_contents to confirm that the files contain the same data.

I'll suggest some functions to write first, then we'll bring it all together:

1. To identify image files, write a function called is_image that takes a path and a list of file extensions, and returns True if the path ends with one of the extensions in the list. Hint: use os.path.splitext—or ask a virtual assistant to write this function for you.

2. Write a function called add_path that takes as arguments a path and a shelf. It should use md5_digest to compute a digest of the file contents. Then it should update the shelf, either creating a new item that maps from the digest to a list containing the path, or appending the path to the list if it exists.

3. Write a function called process_path that takes a path, uses is_image to check whether it's an image file, and uses add_path to add it to the shelf.

When everything is working, you can use the following program to create the shelf, search the *photos* directory and add paths to the shelf, and then check whether there are multiple files with the same digest:

```
db = shelve.open('photos/digests', 'n')
walk('photos', process_path)

for digest, paths in db.items():
    if len(paths) > 1:
        print(paths)
```

You should find one pair of files that have the same digest. Use `same_contents` to check whether they contain the same data.

CHAPTER 14

Classes and Functions

At this point you know how to use functions to organize code and how to use built-in types to organize data. The next step is **object-oriented programming (OOP)**, which uses programmer-defined types to organize both code and data.

Object-oriented programming is a big topic, so we will proceed gradually. In this chapter, we'll start with code that is not idiomatic—that is, it is not the kind of code experienced programmers write—but it is a good place to start. In the next two chapters, we will use additional features to write more idiomatic code.

Programmer-Defined Types

We have used many of Python's built-in types—now we will define a new type. As a first example, we'll create a type called Time that represents a time of day. A programmer-defined type is also called a **class**. A class definition looks like this:

```
class Time:
    """Represents a time of day."""
```

The header indicates that the new class is called Time. The body is a docstring that explains what the class is for. Defining a class creates a **class object**.

The class object is like a factory for creating objects. To create a Time object, you call Time as if it were a function:

```
lunch = Time()
```

The result is a new object whose type is __main__.Time, where __main__ is the name of the module where Time is defined:

```
type(lunch)
```

```
__main__.Time
```

When you print an object, Python tells you what type it is and where it is stored in memory (the prefix 0x means that the following number is in hexadecimal):

```
print(lunch)
```

```
<__main__.Time object at 0x7fbf2c427280>
```

Creating a new object is called **instantiation**, and the object is an **instance** of the class.

Attributes

An object can contain variables, which are called **attributes** and pronounced with the emphasis on the first syllable, as "AT-trib-ute," rather than the second syllable, as "a-TRIB-ute." We can create attributes using dot notation:

```
lunch.hour = 11
lunch.minute = 59
lunch.second = 1
```

This example creates attributes called hour, minute, and second, which contain the hours, minutes, and seconds of the time 11:59:01, which is lunchtime as far as I am concerned.

The following diagram shows the state of lunch and its attributes after these assignments:

The variable lunch refers to a Time object, which contains three attributes. Each attribute refers to an integer. A state diagram like this—which shows an object and its attributes—is called an **object diagram**.

You can read the value of an attribute using the dot operator:

```
lunch.hour
```

```
11
```

You can use an attribute as part of any expression:

```
total_minutes = lunch.hour * 60 + lunch.minute
total_minutes
```

```
719
```

And you can use the dot operator in an expression in an f-string:

```
f'{lunch.hour}:{lunch.minute}:{lunch.second}'
```

```
'11:59:1'
```

But notice that the previous example is not in the standard format. To fix it, we have to print the minute and second attributes with a leading zero. We can do that by extending the expressions in curly braces with a **format specifier**. In the following example, the format specifiers indicate that minute and second should be displayed with at least two digits and a leading zero, if needed:

```
f'{lunch.hour}:{lunch.minute:02d}:{lunch.second:02d}'
```

```
'11:59:01'
```

We'll use this f-string to write a function that displays the value of time objects. You can pass an object as an argument in the usual way. For example, the following function takes a Time object as an argument:

```
def print_time(time):
    s = f'{time.hour:02d}:{time.minute:02d}:{time.second:02d}'
    print(s)
```

When we call it, we can pass lunch as an argument:

```
print_time(lunch)
```

```
11:59:01
```

Objects as Return Values

Functions can return objects. For example, make_time takes parameters called hour, minute, and second, stores them as attributes in a Time object, and returns the new object:

```
def make_time(hour, minute, second):
    time = Time()
    time.hour = hour
    time.minute = minute
    time.second = second
    return time
```

It might be surprising that the parameters have the same names as the attributes, but that's a common way to write a function like this. Here's how we use make_time to create a Time object:

```
time = make_time(11, 59, 1)
print_time(time)
```

```
11:59:01
```

Objects Are Mutable

Suppose you are going to a screening of a movie, like *Monty Python and the Holy Grail*, which starts at 9:20 P.M. and runs for 92 minutes, which is 1 hour and 32 minutes. What time will the movie end?

First, we'll create a Time object that represents the start time:

```
start = make_time(9, 20, 0)
print_time(start)
```

```
09:20:00
```

To find the end time, we can modify the attributes of the Time object, adding the duration of the movie:

```
start.hour += 1
start.minute += 32
print_time(start)
```

```
10:52:00
```

The movie will be over at 10:52 P.M.

Let's encapsulate this computation in a function and generalize it to take the duration of the movie in three parameters: hours, minutes, and seconds:

```
def increment_time(time, hours, minutes, seconds):
    time.hour += hours
    time.minute += minutes
    time.second += seconds
```

Here is an example that demonstrates the effect:

```
start = make_time(9, 20, 0)
increment_time(start, 1, 32, 0)
print_time(start)
```

```
10:52:00
```

The following stack diagram shows the state of the program just before increment_time modifies the object:

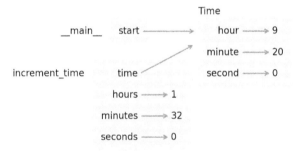

Inside the function, time is an alias for start, so when time is modified, start changes.

This function works, but after it runs, we're left with a variable named start that refers to an object that represents the *end* time, and we no longer have an object that represents the start time. It would be better to leave start unchanged and make a new object to represent the end time. We can do that by copying start and modifying the copy.

Copying

The copy module provides a function called copy that can duplicate any object. We can import it like this:

```
from copy import copy
```

To see how it works, let's start with a new `Time` object that represents the start time of the movie:

```
start = make_time(9, 20, 0)
```

And make a copy:

```
end = copy(start)
```

Now `start` and `end` contain the same data:

```
print_time(start)
print_time(end)

09:20:00
09:20:00
```

But the `is` operator confirms that they are not the same object:

```
start is end

False
```

Let's see what the `==` operator does:

```
start == end

False
```

You might expect `==` to yield `True` because the objects contain the same data. But for programmer-defined classes, the default behavior of the `==` operator is the same as the `is` operator—it checks identity, not equivalence.

Pure Functions

We can use `copy` to write pure functions that don't modify their parameters. For example, here's a function that takes a `Time` object and a duration in hours, minutes, and seconds. It makes a copy of the original object, uses `increment_time` to modify the copy, and returns it:

```
def add_time(time, hours, minutes, seconds):
    total = copy(time)
    increment_time(total, hours, minutes, seconds)
    return total
```

Here's how we use it:

```
end = add_time(start, 1, 32, 0)
print_time(end)
```

```
10:52:00
```

The return value is a new object representing the end time of the movie. And we can confirm that start is unchanged:

```
print_time(start)
```

```
09:20:00
```

add_time is a **pure function** because it does not modify any of the objects passed to it as arguments and its only effect is to return a value.

Anything that can be done with modifiers can also be done with pure functions. In fact, some programming languages only allow pure functions. Programs that use pure functions might be less error prone than programs that use modifiers. But modifiers are sometimes convenient and can be more efficient.

In general, I suggest you write pure functions whenever it is reasonable and resort to modifiers only if there is a compelling advantage. This approach might be called a **functional programming style**.

Prototype and Patch

In the previous example, increment_time and add_time seem to work, but if we try another example, we'll see that they are not quite correct.

Suppose you arrive at the theater and discover that the movie starts at 9:40, not 9:20. Here's what happens when we compute the updated end time:

```
start = make_time(9, 40, 0)
end = add_time(start, 1, 32, 0)
print_time(end)
```

```
10:72:00
```

The result is not a valid time. The problem is that increment_time does not deal with cases where the number of seconds or minutes adds up to more than 60.

Here's an improved version that checks whether second exceeds 60—if so, it increments minute—then checks whether minute exceeds 60—if so, it increments hour:

```
def increment_time(time, hours, minutes, seconds):
    time.hour += hours
    time.minute += minutes
    time.second += seconds

    if time.second >= 60:
        time.second -= 60
        time.minute += 1

    if time.minute >= 60:
        time.minute -= 60
        time.hour += 1
```

Fixing increment_time also fixes add_time, which uses it. So now the previous example works correctly:

```
end = add_time(start, 1, 32, 0)
print_time(end)
```

```
11:12:00
```

But this function is still not correct, because the arguments might be bigger than 60. For example, suppose we are given the run time as 92 minutes, rather than 1 hour and 32 minutes. We might call add_time like this:

```
end = add_time(start, 0, 92, 0)
print_time(end)
```

```
10:72:00
```

The result is not a valid time. So let's try a different approach, using the divmod function. We'll make a copy of start and modify it by incrementing the minute field:

```
end = copy(start)
end.minute = start.minute + 92
end.minute
```

```
132
```

Now minute is 132, which is 2 hours and 12 minutes. We can use divmod to divide by 60 and return the number of whole hours and the number of minutes left over:

```
carry, end.minute = divmod(end.minute, 60)
carry, end.minute
```

```
(2, 12)
```

Now minute is correct, and we can add the hours to hour:

```
end.hour += carry
print_time(end)
```

```
11:12:00
```

The result is a valid time. We can do the same thing with `hour` and `second`, and encapsulate the whole process in a function:

```
def increment_time(time, hours, minutes, seconds):
    time.hour += hours
    time.minute += minutes
    time.second += seconds

    carry, time.second = divmod(time.second, 60)
    carry, time.minute = divmod(time.minute + carry, 60)
    carry, time.hour = divmod(time.hour + carry, 60)
```

With this version of `increment_time`, `add_time` works correctly, even if the arguments exceed `60`:

```
end = add_time(start, 0, 90, 120)
print_time(end)
```

```
11:12:00
```

This section demonstrates a program development plan I call **prototype and patch**. We started with a simple prototype that worked correctly for the first example. Then we tested it with more difficult examples—when we found an error, we modified the program to fix it, like putting a patch on a tire with a puncture.

This approach can be effective, especially if you don't yet have a deep understanding of the problem. But incremental corrections can generate code that is unnecessarily complicated—since it deals with many special cases—and unreliable, since it is hard to know if you have found all the errors.

Design-First Development

An alternative plan is **design-first development**, which involves more planning before prototyping. In a design-first process, sometimes a high-level insight into the problem makes the programming much easier.

In this case, the insight is that we can think of a `Time` object as a 3-digit number in base 60—also known as sexagesimal. The `second` attribute is the "ones column," the `minute` attribute is the "sixties column," and the `hour` attribute is the "thirty-six hundreds column." When we wrote `increment_time`, we were effectively doing addition in base 60, which is why we had to carry from one column to the next.

This observation suggests another approach to the whole problem—we can convert Time objects to integers and take advantage of the fact that Python knows how to do integer arithmetic.

Here is a function that converts from a Time to an integer:

```
def time_to_int(time):
    minutes = time.hour * 60 + time.minute
    seconds = minutes * 60 + time.second
    return seconds
```

The result is the number of seconds since the beginning of the day. For example, 01:01:01 is 1 hour, 1 minute, and 1 second from the beginning of the day, which is the sum of 3600 seconds, 60 seconds, and 1 second:

```
time = make_time(1, 1, 1)
print_time(time)
time_to_int(time)
```

```
01:01:01
```

```
3661
```

And here's a function that goes in the other direction—converting an integer to a Time object—using the divmod function:

```
def int_to_time(seconds):
    minute, second = divmod(seconds, 60)
    hour, minute = divmod(minute, 60)
    return make_time(hour, minute, second)
```

We can test it by converting the previous example back to a Time:

```
time = int_to_time(3661)
print_time(time)
```

```
01:01:01
```

Using these functions, we can write a more concise version of add_time:

```
def add_time(time, hours, minutes, seconds):
    duration = make_time(hours, minutes, seconds)
    seconds = time_to_int(time) + time_to_int(duration)
    return int_to_time(seconds)
```

The first line converts the arguments to a Time object called duration. The second line converts time and duration to seconds and adds them. The third line converts the sum to a Time object and returns it.

Here's how it works:

```
start = make_time(9, 40, 0)
end = add_time(start, 1, 32, 0)
print_time(end)
```

```
11:12:00
```

In some ways, converting from base 60 to base 10 and back is harder than just dealing with times. Base conversion is more abstract; our intuition for dealing with time values is better.

But if we have the insight to treat times as base 60 numbers—and invest the effort to write the conversion functions `time_to_int` and `int_to_time`—we get a program that is shorter, easier to read and debug, and more reliable.

It is also easier to add features later. For example, imagine subtracting two `Time` objects to find the duration between them. The naive approach is to implement subtraction with borrowing. Using the conversion functions is easier and more likely to be correct.

Ironically, sometimes making a problem harder—or more general—makes it easier, because there are fewer special cases and fewer opportunities for error.

Debugging

Python provides several built-in functions that are useful for testing and debugging programs that work with objects. For example, if you are not sure what type an object is, you can ask:

```
type(start)
```

```
__main__.Time
```

You can also use `isinstance` to check whether an object is an instance of a particular class:

```
isinstance(end, Time)
```

```
True
```

If you are not sure whether an object has a particular attribute, you can use the built-in function `hasattr`:

```
hasattr(start, 'hour')
```

```
True
```

To get all of the attributes, and their values, in a dictionary, you can use `vars`:

```
vars(start)
```

```
{'hour': 9, 'minute': 40, 'second': 0}
```

The `structshape` module, which we saw in "Debugging" on page 166, also works with programmer-defined types:

```
from structshape import structshape

t = start, end
structshape(t)
```

```
'tuple of 2 Time'
```

Glossary

object-oriented programming (OOP): A style of programming that uses objects to organize code and data.

class: A programmer-defined type. A class definition creates a new class object.

class object: An object that represents a class—it is the result of a class definition.

instantiation: The process of creating an object that belongs to a class.

instance: An object that belongs to a class.

attribute: A variable associated with an object, also called an instance variable.

object diagram: A graphical representation of an object, its attributes, and their values.

format specifier: In an f-string, a format specifier determines how a value is converted to a string.

pure function: A function that does not modify its parameters or have any effect other than returning a value.

functional programming style: A way of programming that uses pure functions whenever possible.

prototype and patch: A way of developing programs by starting with a rough draft and gradually adding features and fixing bugs.

design-first development: A way of developing programs with more careful planning than prototype and patch.

Exercises

Ask a Virtual Assistant

There is a lot of new vocabulary in this chapter. A conversation with a virtual assistant can help solidify your understanding. Consider asking:

- "What is the difference between a class and a type?"
- "What is the difference between an object and an instance?"
- "What is the difference between a variable and an attribute?"
- "What are the pros and cons of pure functions compared to modifiers?"

Because we are just getting started with object-oriented programming, the code in this chapter is not idiomatic—it is not the kind of code experienced programmers write. If you ask a virtual assistant for help with the exercises, you will probably see features we have not covered yet. In particular, you are likely to see a method called __init__ used to initialize the attributes of an instance.

If these features make sense to you, go ahead and use them. But if not, be patient—we will get there soon. In the meantime, see if you can solve the following exercises using only the features we have covered so far.

Also, in this chapter we saw one example of a format specifier. For more information ask "What format specifiers can be used in a Python f-string?"

Exercise

Write a function called subtract_time that takes two Time objects and returns the interval between them in seconds—assuming that they are two times during the same day.

Exercise

Write a function called `is_after` that takes two `Time` objects and returns `True` if the second time is later in the day than the first, and `False` otherwise:

```
def is_after(t1, t2):
    """Checks whether `t1` is after `t2`.

    >>> is_after(make_time(3, 2, 1), make_time(3, 2, 0))
    True
    >>> is_after(make_time(3, 2, 1), make_time(3, 2, 1))
    False
    >>> is_after(make_time(11, 12, 0), make_time(9, 40, 0))
    True
    """

    return None
```

Exercise

Here's a definition for a `Date` class that represents a date—that is, a year, month, and day of the month:

```
class Date:
    """Represents a year, month, and day"""
```

1. Write a function called `make_date` that takes `year`, `month`, and `day` as parameters, makes a `Date` object, assigns the parameters to attributes, and returns the result as the new object. Create an object that represents June 22, 1933.

2. Write a function called `print_date` that takes a `Date` object, uses an f-string to format the attributes, and prints the result. If you test it with the `Date` you created, the result should be `1933-06-22`.

3. Write a function called `is_after` that takes two `Date` objects as parameters and returns `True` if the first comes after the second. Create a second object that represents September 17, 1933, and check whether it comes after the first object.

Hint: you might find it useful to write a function called `date_to_tuple` that takes a `Date` object and returns a tuple that contains its attributes in year, month, day order.

CHAPTER 15

Classes and Methods

Python is an **object-oriented language**—that is, it provides features that support object-oriented programming, which has these defining characteristics:

- Most of the computation is expressed in terms of operations on objects.
- Objects often represent things in the real world, and methods often correspond to the ways things in the real world interact.
- Programs include class and method definitions.

For example, in the previous chapter we defined a Time class that corresponds to the way people record the time of day, and we defined functions that correspond to the kinds of things people do with times. But there was no explicit connection between the definition of the Time class and the function definitions that follow. We can make the connection explicit by rewriting a function as a **method**, which is defined inside a class definition.

Defining Methods

In the previous chapter, we defined a class named Time and wrote a function named print_time that displays a time of day:

```
class Time:
    """Represents the time of day."""

def print_time(time):
    s = f'{time.hour:02d}:{time.minute:02d}:{time.second:02d}'
    print(s)
```

To make print_time a method, all we have to do is move the function definition inside the class definition. Notice the change in indentation.

At the same time, we'll change the name of the parameter from `time` to `self`. This change is not necessary, but it is conventional for the first parameter of a method to be named `self`:

```
class Time:
    """Represents the time of day."""

    def print_time(self):
        s = f'{self.hour:02d}:{self.minute:02d}:{self.second:02d}'
        print(s)
```

To call this function, you have to pass a `Time` object as an argument. Here's the function we'll use to make a `Time` object:

```
def make_time(hour, minute, second):
    time = Time()
    time.hour = hour
    time.minute = minute
    time.second = second
    return time
```

And here's a `Time` instance:

```
start = make_time(9, 40, 0)
```

There are two ways to call `print_time`. The first (and less common) way is to use function syntax:

```
Time.print_time(start)
```

```
09:40:00
```

In this version, `Time` is the name of the class, `print_time` is the name of the method, and `start` is passed as a parameter. The second (and more idiomatic) way is to use the method syntax:

```
start.print_time()
```

```
09:40:00
```

In this version, `start` is the object the method is invoked on, which is called the **receiver**, based on the analogy that invoking a method is like sending a message to an object.

Regardless of the syntax, the behavior of the method is the same. The receiver is assigned to the first parameter, so inside the method, `self` refers to the same object as `start`.

Another Method

Here's the `time_to_int` function from Chapter 14:

```
def time_to_int(time):
    minutes = time.hour * 60 + time.minute
    seconds = minutes * 60 + time.second
    return seconds
```

And here's a version rewritten as a method:

```
%%add_method_to Time

    def time_to_int(self):
        minutes = self.hour * 60 + self.minute
        seconds = minutes * 60 + self.second
        return seconds
```

The first line uses the special command `add_method_to`, which adds a method to a previously defined class. This command works in a Jupyter notebook, but it is not part of Python, so it won't work in other environments. Normally, all methods of a class are inside the class definition, so they get defined at the same time as the class. But for this book, it is helpful to define one method at a time.

As in the previous example, the method definition is indented and the name of the parameter is `self`. Other than that, the method is identical to the function. Here's how we invoke it:

```
start.time_to_int()
```

```
34800
```

It is common to say that we "call" a function and "invoke" a method, but they mean the same thing.

Static Methods

As another example, let's consider the `int_to_time` function. Here's the version from Chapter 14:

```
def int_to_time(seconds):
    minute, second = divmod(seconds, 60)
    hour, minute = divmod(minute, 60)
    return make_time(hour, minute, second)
```

This function takes `seconds` as a parameter and returns a new `Time` object. If we transform it into a method of the `Time` class, we have to invoke it on a `Time` object. But if we're trying to create a new `Time` object, what are we supposed to invoke it on?

We can solve this chicken-and-egg problem using a **static method**, which is a method that does not require an instance of the class to be invoked. Here's how we rewrite this function as a static method:

```
%%add_method_to Time

def int_to_time(seconds):
    minute, second = divmod(seconds, 60)
    hour, minute = divmod(minute, 60)
    return make_time(hour, minute, second)
```

Because it is a static method, it does not have `self` as a parameter. To invoke it, we use `Time`, which is the class object:

```
start = Time.int_to_time(34800)
```

The result is a new object that represents `9:40`:

```
start.print_time()
```

```
09:40:00
```

Now that we have `Time.from_seconds`, we can use it to write `add_time` as a method. Here's the function from the previous chapter:

```
def add_time(time, hours, minutes, seconds):
    duration = make_time(hours, minutes, seconds)
    seconds = time_to_int(time) + time_to_int(duration)
    return int_to_time(seconds)
```

And here's a version rewritten as a method:

```
%%add_method_to Time

def add_time(self, hours, minutes, seconds):
    duration = make_time(hours, minutes, seconds)
    seconds = time_to_int(self) + time_to_int(duration)
    return Time.int_to_time(seconds)
```

`add_time` has `self` as a parameter because it is not a static method. It is an ordinary method—also called an **instance method**. To invoke it, we need a `Time` instance:

```
end = start.add_time(1, 32, 0)
print_time(end)
```

```
11:12:00
```

Comparing Time Objects

As one more example, let's write `is_after` as a method. Here's the `is_after` function, which is a solution to an exercise in Chapter 14:

```
def is_after(t1, t2):
    return time_to_int(t1) > time_to_int(t2)
```

And here it is as a method:

```
%%add_method_to Time

    def is_after(self, other):
        return self.time_to_int() > other.time_to_int()
```

Because we're comparing two objects, and the first parameter is `self`, we'll call the second parameter `other`. To use this method, we have to invoke it on one object and pass the other as an argument:

```
end.is_after(start)
```

```
True
```

One nice thing about this syntax is that it almost reads like a question, "`end` is after `start`?"

The __str__ Method

When you write a method, you can choose almost any name you want. However, some names have special meanings. For example, if an object has a method named __str__, Python uses that method to convert the object to a string. For example, here is a __str__ method for a Time object:

```
%%add_method_to Time

    def __str__(self):
        s = f'{self.hour:02d}:{self.minute:02d}:{self.second:02d}'
        return s
```

This method is similar to `print_time` from Chapter 14, except that it returns the string rather than printing it.

You can invoke this method in the usual way:

```
end.__str__()
```

```
'11:12:00'
```

But Python can also invoke it for you. If you use the built-in function `str` to convert a `Time` object to a string, Python uses the `__str__` method in the `Time` class:

```
str(end)
```

```
'11:12:00'
```

And it does the same if you print a `Time` object:

```
print(end)
```

```
11:12:00
```

Methods like `__str__` are called **special methods**. You can identify them because their names begin and end with two underscores.

The __init__ Method

The most special of the special methods is `__init__`, so-called because it initializes the attributes of a new object. An `__init__` method for the `Time` class might look like this:

```
%%add_method_to Time

    def __init__(self, hour=0, minute=0, second=0):
        self.hour = hour
        self.minute = minute
        self.second = second
```

Now when we instantiate a `Time` object, Python invokes `__init__`, and passes along the arguments. So we can create an object and initialize the attributes at the same time:

```
time = Time(9, 40, 0)
print(time)
```

```
09:40:00
```

In this example, the parameters are optional, so if you call `Time` with no arguments, you get the default values:

```
time = Time()
print(time)
```

```
00:00:00
```

If you provide one argument, it overrides `hour`:

```
time = Time(9)
print(time)
```

```
09:00:00
```

If you provide two arguments, they override `hour` and `minute`:

```
time = Time(9, 45)
print(time)
```

```
09:45:00
```

And if you provide three arguments, they override all three default values.

When I write a new class, I almost always start by writing `__init__`, which makes it easier to create objects, and `__str__`, which is useful for debugging.

Operator Overloading

By defining other special methods, you can specify the behavior of operators on programmer-defined types. For example, if you define a method named `__add__` for the `Time` class, you can use the + operator on `Time` objects.

Here is an `__add__` method:

```
%%add_method_to Time

    def __add__(self, other):
        seconds = self.time_to_int() + other.time_to_int()
        return Time.int_to_time(seconds)
```

We can use it like this:

```
duration = Time(1, 32)
end = start + duration
print(end)
```

```
11:12:00
```

There is a lot happening when we run these three lines of code:

- When we instantiate a Time object, the __init__ method is invoked.
- When we use the + operator with a Time object, its __add__ method is invoked.
- And when we print a Time object, its __str__ method is invoked.

Changing the behavior of an operator so that it works with programmer-defined types is called **operator overloading**. For every operator, like +, there is a corresponding special method, like __add__.

Debugging

A Time object is valid if the values of minute and second are between 0 and 60—including 0 but not 60—and if hour is positive. Also, hour and minute should be integer values, but we might allow second to have a fraction part. Requirements like these are called **invariants** because they should always be true. To put it a different way, if they are not true, something has gone wrong.

Writing code to check invariants can help detect errors and find their causes. For example, you might have a method like is_valid that takes a Time object and returns False if it violates an invariant:

```
%%add_method_to Time

    def is_valid(self):
        if self.hour < 0 or self.minute < 0 or self.second < 0:
            return False
        if self.minute >= 60 or self.second >= 60:
            return False
        if not isinstance(self.hour, int):
            return False
        if not isinstance(self.minute, int):
            return False
        return True
```

Then, at the beginning of each method you can check the arguments to make sure they are valid:

```
%%add_method_to Time

    def is_after(self, other):
        assert self.is_valid(), 'self is not a valid Time'
        assert other.is_valid(), 'self is not a valid Time'
        return self.time_to_int() > other.time_to_int()
```

The `assert` statement evaluates the expression that follows. If the result is `True`, it does nothing; if the result is `False`, it causes an `AssertionError`. Here's an example:

```
duration = Time(minute=132)
print(duration)
```

```
00:132:00
```

```
start.is_after(duration)
```

```
AssertionError: self is not a valid Time
```

`assert` statements are useful because they distinguish code that deals with normal conditions from code that checks for errors.

Glossary

object-oriented language: A language that provides features to support object-oriented programming, notably user-defined types and inheritance.

method: A function that is defined inside a class definition and is invoked on instances of that class.

receiver: The object a method is invoked on.

static method: A method that can be invoked without an object as receiver.

instance method: A method that must be invoked with an object as receiver.

special method: A method that changes the way operators and some functions work with an object.

operator overloading: The process of using special methods to change the way operators work with user-defined types.

invariant: A condition that should always be true during the execution of a program.

Exercises

Ask a Virtual Assistant

For more information about static methods, ask a virtual assistant:

- "What's the difference between an instance method and a static method?"
- "Why are static methods called static?"

If you ask a virtual assistant to generate a static method, the result will probably begin with @staticmethod, which is a "decorator" that indicates that it is a static method. Decorators are not covered in this book, but if you are curious, you can ask a virtual assistant for more information.

In this chapter we rewrote several functions as methods. Virtual assistants are generally good at this kind of code transformation. As an example, paste the following function into a virtual assistant and ask it, "Rewrite this function as a method of the Time class."

```
def subtract_time(t1, t2):
    return time_to_int(t1) - time_to_int(t2)
```

Exercise

In Chapter 14, a series of exercises asked you to write a Date class and several functions that work with Date objects. Now let's practice rewriting those functions as methods:

1. Write a definition for a Date class that represents a date—that is, a year, month, and day of the month.

2. Write an __init__ method that takes year, month, and day as parameters and assigns the parameters to attributes. Create an object that represents June 22, 1933.

3. Write a __str__ method that uses a format string to format the attributes and returns the result. If you test it with the Date you created, the result should be 1933-06-22.

4. Write a method called is_after that takes two Date objects and returns True if the first comes after the second. Create a second object that represents September 17, 1933, and check whether it comes after the first object.

Hint: you might find it useful to write a method called to_tuple that returns a tuple that contains the attributes of a Date object in year-month-day order.

CHAPTER 16

Classes and Objects

At this point we have defined classes and created objects that represent the time of day and the day of the year. And we've defined methods that create, modify, and perform computations with these objects.

In this chapter we'll continue our tour of object-oriented programming (OOP) by defining classes that represent geometric objects, including points, lines, rectangles, and circles. We'll write methods that create and modify these objects, and we'll use the `jupyturtle` module to draw them.

I'll use these classes to demonstrate OOP topics including object identity and equivalence, shallow and deep copying, and polymorphism.

Creating a Point

In computer graphics, a location on the screen is often represented using a pair of coordinates in an x-y plane. By convention, the point (`0, 0`) usually represents the upper-left corner of the screen, and (`x, y`) represents the point x units to the right and y units down from the origin. Compared to the Cartesian coordinate system you might have seen in a math class, the y-axis is upside down.

There are several ways we might represent a point in Python:

- We can store the coordinates separately in two variables, x and y.
- We can store the coordinates as elements in a list or tuple.
- We can create a new type to represent points as objects.

In object-oriented programming, it would be most idiomatic to create a new type. To do that, we'll start with a class definition for `Point`:

```
class Point:
    """Represents a point in 2-D space."""

    def __init__(self, x, y):
        self.x = x
        self.y = y

    def __str__(self):
        return f'Point({self.x}, {self.y})'
```

The `__init__` method takes the coordinates as parameters and assigns them to attributes x and y. The `__str__` method returns a string representation of the `Point`.

Now we can instantiate and display a `Point` object like this:

```
start = Point(0, 0)
print(start)
```

```
Point(0, 0)
```

The following diagram shows the state of the new object:

```
              Point
start ────▶   x ───▶ 0

              y ───▶ 0
```

As usual, a programmer-defined type is represented by a box with the name of the type outside and the attributes inside.

In general, programmer-defined types are mutable, so we can write a method like `translate` that takes two numbers, dx and dy, and adds them to the attributes x and y:

```
%%add_method_to Point

    def translate(self, dx, dy):
        self.x += dx
        self.y += dy
```

This function translates the `Point` from one location in the plane to another.

If we don't want to modify an existing `Point`, we can use `copy` to copy the original object and then modify the copy:

```
from copy import copy

end1 = copy(start)
end1.translate(300, 0)
print(end1)
```

```
Point(300, 0)
```

We can encapsulate those steps in another method called `translated`:

```
%%add_method_to Point

    def translated(self, dx=0, dy=0):
        point = copy(self)
        point.translate(dx, dy)
        return point
```

In the same way that the built-in function `sort` modifies a list, and the `sorted` function creates a new list, now we have a `translate` method that modifies a `Point`, and a `translated` method that creates a new one.

Here's an example:

```
end2 = start.translated(0, 150)
print(end2)
```

```
Point(0, 150)
```

In the next section, we'll use these points to define and draw a line.

Creating a Line

Now let's define a class that represents the line segment between two points. As usual, we'll start with an __init__ method and a __str__ method:

```
class Line:
    def __init__(self, p1, p2):
        self.p1 = p1
        self.p2 = p2

    def __str__(self):
        return f'Line({self.p1}, {self.p2})'
```

With those two methods, we can instantiate and display a `Line` object we'll use to represent the x-axis:

```
line1 = Line(start, end1)
print(line1)
```

```
Line(Point(0, 0), Point(300, 0))
```

When we call `print` and pass `line` as a parameter, `print` invokes `__str__` on `line`. The `__str__` method uses an f-string to create a string representation of the `line`.

The f-string contains two expressions in curly braces, `self.p1` and `self.p2`. When those expressions are evaluated, the results are `Point` objects. Then, when they are converted to strings, the `__str__` method from the `Point` class gets invoked.

That's why, when we display a `Line`, the result contains the string representations of the `Point` objects.

The following object diagram shows the state of this `Line` object:

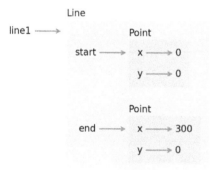

String representations and object diagrams are useful for debugging, but the point of this example is to generate graphics, not text! So we'll use the `jupyturtle` module to draw lines on the screen.

As we did in "The jupyturtle Module" on page 39, we'll use `make_turtle` to create a `Turtle` object and a small canvas where it can draw. To draw lines, we'll use two new functions from the `jupyturtle` module:

jumpto

    Takes two coordinates and moves the `Turtle` to the given location without drawing a line

moveto

    Moves the `Turtle` from its current location to the given location, and draws a line segment between them

Here's how we import them:

```
from jupyturtle import make_turtle, jumpto, moveto
```

And here's a method that draws a `Line`:

```
%%add_method_to Line

    def draw(self):
        jumpto(self.p1.x, self.p1.y)
        moveto(self.p2.x, self.p2.y)
```

To show how it's used, I'll create a second line that represents the y-axis:

```
line2 = Line(start, end2)
print(line2)
```

```
Line(Point(0, 0), Point(0, 150))
```

And then draw the axes:

```
make_turtle()
line1.draw()
line2.draw()
```

As we define and draw more objects, we'll use these lines again. But first let's talk about object equivalence and identity.

Equivalence and Identity

Suppose we create two points with the same coordinates:

```
p1 = Point(200, 100)
p2 = Point(200, 100)
```

If we use the == operator to compare them, we get the default behavior for programmer-defined types—the result is True only if they are the same object, which they are not:

```
p1 == p2
```

```
False
```

If we want to change that behavior, we can provide a special method called __eq__ that defines what it means for two Point objects to be equal:

```
%%add_method_to Point

def __eq__(self, other):
    return (self.x == other.x) and (self.y == other.y)
```

This definition considers two Points to be equal if their attributes are equal. Now when we use the == operator, it invokes the __eq__ method, which indicates that p1 and p2 are considered equal:

```
p1 == p2
```

```
True
```

But the is operator still indicates that they are different objects:

```
p1 is p2
```

```
False
```

It's not possible to override the is operator—it always checks whether the objects are **identical**. But for programmer-defined types, you can override the == operator so it checks whether the objects are **equivalent**. And you can define what equivalent means.

Creating a Rectangle

Now let's define a class that represents and draws rectangles. To keep things simple, we'll assume that the rectangles are either vertical or horizontal, not at an angle. What attributes do you think we should use to specify the location and size of a rectangle?

There are at least two possibilities:

- You could specify the width and height of the rectangle and the location of one corner.

- You could specify two opposing corners.

At this point it's hard to say whether one is better than the other, so let's implement the first one. Here is the class definition:

```
class Rectangle:
    """Represents a rectangle.

    attributes: width, height, corner.
    """
    def __init__(self, width, height, corner):
        self.width = width
        self.height = height
        self.corner = corner

    def __str__(self):
        return f'Rectangle({self.width}, {self.height}, {self.corner})'
```

As usual, the __init__ method assigns the parameters to attributes and the __str__ returns a string representation of the object. Now we can instantiate a Rectangle object, using a Point as the location of the upper-left corner:

```
corner = Point(30, 20)
box1 = Rectangle(100, 50, corner)
print(box1)
```

```
Rectangle(100, 50, Point(30, 20))
```

The following diagram shows the state of this object:

To draw a rectangle, we'll use the following method to make four Point objects to represent the corners:

```
%%add_method_to Rectangle

def make_points(self):
    p1 = self.corner
    p2 = p1.translated(self.width, 0)
    p3 = p2.translated(0, self.height)
    p4 = p3.translated(-self.width, 0)
    return p1, p2, p3, p4
```

Then we'll make four `Line` objects to represent the sides:

```
%%add_method_to Rectangle

    def make_lines(self):
        p1, p2, p3, p4 = self.make_points()
        return Line(p1, p2), Line(p2, p3), Line(p3, p4), Line(p4, p1)
```

Then we'll draw the sides:

```
%%add_method_to Rectangle

    def draw(self):
        lines = self.make_lines()
        for line in lines:
            line.draw()
```

Here's an example:

```
make_turtle()
line1.draw()
line2.draw()
box1.draw()
```

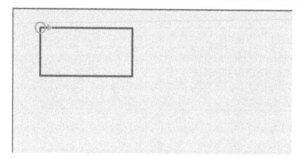

The figure includes two lines to represent the axes.

Changing Rectangles

Now let's consider two methods that modify rectangles, `grow` and `translate`. We'll see that `grow` works as expected, but `translate` has a subtle bug. See if you can figure it out before I explain.

`grow` takes two numbers, `dwidth` and `dheight`, and adds them to the `width` and
height attributes of the rectangle:

```
%%add_method_to Rectangle

    def grow(self, dwidth, dheight):
        self.width += dwidth
        self.height += dheight
```

Here's an example that demonstrates the effect by making a copy of `box1` and invoking `grow` on the copy:

```
box2 = copy(box1)
box2.grow(60, 40)
print(box2)
```

```
Rectangle(160, 90, Point(30, 20))
```

If we draw `box1` and `box2`, we can confirm that `grow` works as expected:

```
make_turtle()
line1.draw()
line2.draw()
box1.draw()
box2.draw()
```

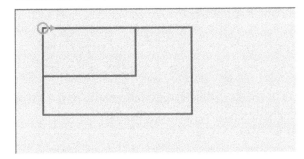

Now let's see about `translate`. It takes two numbers, dx and dy, and moves the rectangle the given distances in the x and y directions:

```
%%add_method_to Rectangle

    def translate(self, dx, dy):
        self.corner.translate(dx, dy)
```

To demonstrate the effect, we'll translate box2 to the right and down:

```
box2.translate(30, 20)
print(box2)
```

```
Rectangle(160, 90, Point(60, 40))
```

Now let's see what happens if we draw box1 and box2 again:

```
make_turtle()
line1.draw()
line2.draw()
box1.draw()
box2.draw()
```

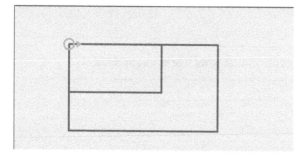

It looks like both rectangles moved, which is not what we intended! The next section explains what went wrong.

Deep Copy

When we use copy to duplicate box1, it copies the Rectangle object but not the Point object it contains. So box1 and box2 are different objects, as intended:

```
box1 is box2
```

```
False
```

But their corner attributes refer to the same object:

```
box1.corner is box2.corner
```

```
True
```

The following diagram shows the state of these objects:

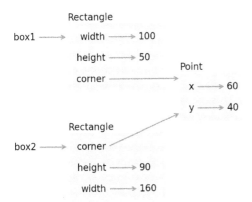

What copy does is create a **shallow copy** because it copies the object but not the objects it contains. As a result, changing the width or height of one Rectangle does not affect the other, but changing the attributes of the shared Point affects both! This behavior is confusing and error prone.

Fortunately, the copy module provides another function, called deepcopy, that copies not only the object but also the objects it refers to, and the objects *they* refer to, and so on. This operation is called a **deep copy**.

To demonstrate, let's start with a new Rectangle that contains a new Point:

```
corner = Point(20, 20)
box3 = Rectangle(100, 50, corner)
print(box3)
```

```
Rectangle(100, 50, Point(20, 20))
```

And we'll make a deep copy:

```
from copy import deepcopy

box4 = deepcopy(box3)
```

We can confirm that the two Rectangle objects refer to different Point objects:

```
box3.corner is box4.corner
```

```
False
```

Because box3 and box4 are completely separate objects, we can modify one without affecting the other. To demonstrate, we'll move box3 and grow box4:

```
box3.translate(50, 30)
box4.grow(100, 60)
```

And we can confirm that the effect is as expected:

```
make_turtle()
line1.draw()
line2.draw()
box3.draw()
box4.draw()
```

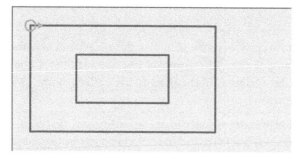

Polymorphism

In the previous example, we invoked the draw method on two Line objects and two Rectangle objects. We can do the same thing more concisely by making a list of objects:

```
shapes = [line1, line2, box3, box4]
```

The elements of this list are different types, but they all provide a draw method, so we can loop through the list and invoke draw on each one:

```
make_turtle()

for shape in shapes:
    shape.draw()
```

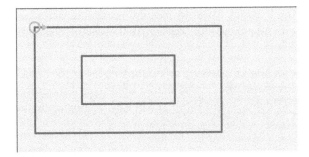

The first and second time through the loop, `shape` refers to a `Line` object, so when `draw` is invoked, the method that runs is the one defined in the `Line` class.

The third and fourth time through the loop, `shape` refers to a `Rectangle` object, so when `draw` is invoked, the method that runs is the one defined in the `Rectangle` class.

In a sense, each object knows how to draw itself. This feature is called **polymorphism**. The word comes from Greek roots that mean "many shaped." In object-oriented programming, polymorphism is the ability of different types to provide the same methods, which makes it possible to perform many computations—like drawing shapes—by invoking the same method on different types of objects.

As an exercise at the end of this chapter, you'll define a new class that represents a circle and provides a `draw` method. Then you can use polymorphism to draw lines, rectangles, and circles.

Debugging

In this chapter, we ran into a subtle bug that happened because we created a `Point` that was shared by two `Rectangle` objects, and then we modified the `Point`. In general, there are two ways to avoid problems like this: you can avoid sharing objects or you can avoid modifying them.

To avoid sharing objects, you can use deep copy, as we did in this chapter.

To avoid modifying objects, consider replacing modifiers like `translate` with pure functions like `translated`. For example, here's a version of `translated` that creates a new `Point` and never modifies its attributes:

```
def translated(self, dx=0, dy=0):
    x = self.x + dx
    y = self.y + dy
    return Point(x, y)
```

Python provides features that make it easier to avoid modifying objects. They are beyond the scope of this book, but if you are curious, ask a virtual assistant, "How do I make a Python object immutable?"

Creating a new object takes more time than modifying an existing one, but the difference seldom matters in practice. Programs that avoid shared objects and modifiers are often easier to develop, test, and debug—and the best kind of debugging is the kind you don't have to do.

Glossary

identical: Being the same object (which implies equivalence).

equivalent: Having the same value.

shallow copy: A copy operation that does not copy nested objects.

deep copy: A copy operation that also copies nested objects.

polymorphism: The ability of a method or operator to work with multiple types of objects.

Exercises

Ask a Virtual Assistant

For all of the following exercises, consider asking a virtual assistant for help. If you do, you'll want include as part of the prompt the class definitions for Point, Line, and Rectangle—otherwise the virtual assistant will make a guess about their attributes and functions, and the code it generates won't work.

Exercise

Write an __eq__ method for the Line class that returns True if the Line objects refer to Point objects that are equivalent, in either order.

Exercise

Write a Line method called midpoint that computes the midpoint of a line segment and returns the result as a Point object.

Exercise

Write a Rectangle method called midpoint that finds the point in the center of a rectangle and returns the result as a Point object.

Exercise

Write a Rectangle method called make_cross that does the following:

1. Uses make_lines to get a list of Line objects that represent the four sides of the rectangle.

2. Computes the midpoints of the four lines.

3. Makes and returns a list of two Line objects that represent lines connecting opposite midpoints, forming a cross through the middle of the rectangle.

Exercise

Write a definition for a class named Circle with attributes center and radius, where center is a Point object and radius is a number. Include special methods __init__ and a __str__, and a method called draw that uses jupyturtle functions to draw the circle.

CHAPTER 17

Inheritance

The language feature most often associated with object-oriented programming is **inheritance**. Inheritance is the ability to define a new class that is a modified version of an existing class. In this chapter I demonstrate inheritance using classes that represent playing cards, decks of cards, and poker hands. If you don't play poker, don't worry—I'll tell you what you need to know.

Representing Cards

There are 52 playing cards in a standard deck—each of them belongs to one of four suits and one of thirteen ranks. The suits are Spades, Hearts, Diamonds, and Clubs. The ranks are Ace, 2, 3, 4, 5, 6, 7, 8, 9, 10, Jack, Queen, and King. Depending on which game you are playing, an Ace can be higher than King or lower than 2.

If we want to define a new object to represent a playing card, it is obvious what the attributes should be: `rank` and `suit`. It is less obvious what type the attributes should be. One possibility is to use strings like `'Spade'` for suits and `'Queen'` for ranks. A problem with this implementation is that it would not be easy to compare cards to see which has a higher rank or suit.

An alternative is to use integers to **encode** the ranks and suits. In this context, "encode" means that we are going to define a mapping between numbers and suits, or between numbers and ranks. This kind of encoding is not meant to be a secret (that would be "encryption").

For example, this table shows the suits and the corresponding integer codes:

Suit	Code
Spades	3
Hearts	2
Diamonds	1
Clubs	0

With this encoding, we can compare suits by comparing their codes.

To encode the ranks, we'll use the integer 2 to represent the rank 2, 3 to represent 3, and so on up to 10. The following table shows the codes for the face cards:

Rank	Code
Jack	11
Queen	12
King	13

And we can use either 1 or 14 to represent an Ace, depending on whether we want it to be considered lower or higher than the other ranks.

To represent these encodings, we will use two lists of strings, one with the names of the suits and the other with the names of the ranks.

Here's a definition for a class that represents a playing card, with these lists of strings as **class variables**, which are variables defined inside a class definition, but not inside a method:

```python
class Card:
    """Represents a standard playing card."""

    suit_names = ['Clubs', 'Diamonds', 'Hearts', 'Spades']
    rank_names = [None, 'Ace', '2', '3', '4', '5', '6', '7',
                  '8', '9', '10', 'Jack', 'Queen', 'King', 'Ace']
```

The first element of rank_names is None because there is no card with rank zero. By including None as a place keeper, we get a list with the nice property that the index 2 maps to the string '2', and so on.

Class variables are associated with the class, rather than an instance of the class, so we can access them like this:

```python
Card.suit_names
```

```
['Clubs', 'Diamonds', 'Hearts', 'Spades']
```

We can use `suit_names` to look up a suit and get the corresponding string:

```
Card.suit_names[0]
```

```
'Clubs'
```

And use `rank_names` to look up a rank:

```
Card.rank_names[11]
```

```
'Jack'
```

Card Attributes

Here's an `__init__` method for the `Card` class—it takes `suit` and `rank` as parameters and assigns them to attributes with the same names:

```
%%add_method_to Card

    def __init__(self, suit, rank):
        self.suit = suit
        self.rank = rank
```

Now we can create a `Card` object like this:

```
queen = Card(1, 12)
```

We can use the new instance to access the attributes:

```
queen.suit, queen.rank
```

```
(1, 12)
```

It is also legal to use the instance to access the class variables:

```
queen.suit_names
```

```
['Clubs', 'Diamonds', 'Hearts', 'Spades']
```

But if you use the class, it is clearer that they are class variables, not attributes.

Printing Cards

Here's a __str__ method for Card objects:

```
%%add_method_to Card

    def __str__(self):
        rank_name = Card.rank_names[self.rank]
        suit_name = Card.suit_names[self.suit]
        return f'{rank_name} of {suit_name}'
```

When we print a Card, Python calls the __str__ method to get a human-readable representation of the card:

```
print(queen)
```

```
Queen of Diamonds
```

The following is a diagram of the Card class object and the Card instance. Card is a class object, so its type is type. queen is an instance of Card, so its type is Card. To save space, I didn't draw the contents of suit_names and rank_names:

```
                 type                list
Card ──────►     suit_names ──────►

                                     list
                 rank_names ──────►


                 Card
queen ──────►    suit ──────► 1

                 rank ──────► 11
```

Every Card instance has its own suit and rank attributes, but there is only one Card class object, and only one copy of the class variables suit_names and rank_names.

Comparing Cards

Suppose we create a second Card object with the same suit and rank:

```
queen2 = Card(1, 12)
print(queen2)
```

```
Queen of Diamonds
```

If we use the == operator to compare them, it checks whether queen and queen2 refer to the same object:

```
queen == queen2
```

```
False
```

They don't, so it returns False. We can change this behavior by defining a special method called __eq__:

```
%%add_method_to Card

    def __eq__(self, other):
        return self.suit == other.suit and self.rank == other.rank
```

```
"Class 'Card' not found."
```

__eq__ takes two Card objects as parameters and returns True if they have the same suit and rank, even if they are not the same object. In other words, it checks whether they are equivalent, even if they are not identical.

When we use the == operator with Card objects, Python calls the __eq__ method:

```
queen == queen2
```

```
True
```

As a second test, let's create a card with the same suit and a different rank:

```
six = Card(1, 6)
print(six)
```

```
6 of Diamonds
```

We can confirm that queen and six are not equivalent:

```
queen == six
```

```
False
```

If we use the != operator, Python invokes a special method called __ne__, if it exists. Otherwise, it invokes __eq__ and inverts the result—so if __eq__ returns True, the result of the != operator is False:

```
queen != queen2
```

False

```
queen != six
```

True

Now suppose we want to compare two cards to see which is bigger. If we use one of the relational operators, we get a TypeError:

```
queen < queen2
```

TypeError: '<' not supported between instances of 'Card' and 'Card'

To change the behavior of the < operator, we can define a special method called __lt__, which is short for "less than." For the sake of this example, let's assume that suit is more important than rank—so all Spades outrank all Hearts, which outrank all Diamonds, and so on. If two cards have the same suit, the one with the higher rank wins.

To implement this logic, we'll use the following method, which returns a tuple containing a card's suit and rank, in that order:

```
%%add_method_to Card

    def to_tuple(self):
        return (self.suit, self.rank)
```

We can use this method to write __lt__:

```
%%add_method_to Card

    def __lt__(self, other):
        return self.to_tuple() < other.to_tuple()
```

Tuple comparison compares the first elements from each tuple, which represent the suits. If they are the same, it compares the second elements, which represent the ranks.

Now if we use the < operator, it invokes the __lt__ operator:

```
six < queen
```

True

If we use the > operator, it invokes a special method called `__gt__`, if it exists. Otherwise it invokes `__lt__` with the arguments in the opposite order:

```
queen < queen2
```

```
False
```

```
queen > queen2
```

```
False
```

Finally, if we use the <= operator, it invokes a special method called `__le__`:

```
%%add_method_to Card

    def __le__(self, other):
        return self.to_tuple() <= other.to_tuple()
```

So we can check whether one card is less than or equal to another:

```
queen <= queen2
```

```
True
```

```
queen <= six
```

```
False
```

If we use the >= operator, it uses `__ge__` if it exists. Otherwise, it invokes `__le__` with the arguments in the opposite order:

```
queen >= six
```

```
True
```

As we have defined them, these methods are complete in the sense that we can compare any two `Card` objects, and consistent in the sense that results from different operators don't contradict each other. With these two properties, we can say that `Card` objects are **totally ordered**. And that means, as we'll see soon, that they can be sorted.

Decks

Now that we have objects that represent cards, let's define objects that represent decks. The following is a class definition for `Deck` with an `__init__` method that takes a list of `Card` objects as a parameter and assigns it to an attribute called `cards`:

```
class Deck:

    def __init__(self, cards):
        self.cards = cards
```

To create a list that contains the 52 cards in a standard deck, we'll use the following static method:

```
%%add_method_to Deck

    def make_cards():
        cards = []
        for suit in range(4):
            for rank in range(2, 15):
                card = Card(suit, rank)
                cards.append(card)
        return cards
```

In `make_cards`, the outer loop enumerates the suits from 0 to 3. The inner loop enumerates the ranks from 2 to 14—where 14 represents an Ace that outranks a King. Each iteration creates a new `Card` with the current suit and rank, and appends it to `cards`. Here's how we make a list of cards and a `Deck` object that contains it:

```
cards = Deck.make_cards()
deck = Deck(cards)
len(deck.cards)
```

```
52
```

It contains 52 cards, as intended.

Printing the Deck

Here is a `__str__` method for `Deck`:

```
%%add_method_to Deck

    def __str__(self):
        res = []
        for card in self.cards:
            res.append(str(card))
        return '\n'.join(res)
```

This method demonstrates an efficient way to accumulate a large string—building a list of strings and then using the string method `join`.

We'll test this method with a deck that only contains two cards:

```
small_deck = Deck([queen, six])
```

If we call `str`, it invokes `__str__`:

```
str(small_deck)
```

```
'Queen of Diamonds\n6 of Diamonds'
```

When Jupyter displays a string, it shows the "representational" form of the string, which represents a newline with the sequence \n.

However, if we print the result, Jupyter shows the "printable" form of the string, which prints the newline as whitespace:

```
print(small_deck)
```

```
Queen of Diamonds
6 of Diamonds
```

So the cards appear on separate lines.

Add, Remove, Shuffle, and Sort

To deal cards, we would like a method that removes a card from the deck and returns it. The list method pop provides a convenient way to do that:

```
%%add_method_to Deck

    def take_card(self):
        return self.cards.pop()
```

Here's how we use it:

```
card = deck.take_card()
print(card)
```

```
Ace of Spades
```

We can confirm that there are 51 cards left in the deck:

```
len(deck.cards)
```

51

To add a card, we can use the list method append:

```
%%add_method_to Deck

    def put_card(self, card):
        self.cards.append(card)
```

As an example, we can put back the card we just popped:

```
deck.put_card(card)
len(deck.cards)
```

52

To shuffle the deck, we can use the shuffle function from the random module:

```
import random
```

```
%%add_method_to Deck

    def shuffle(self):
        random.shuffle(self.cards)
```

If we shuffle the deck and print the first few cards, we can see that they are in no apparent order:

```
deck.shuffle()
for card in deck.cards[:4]:
    print(card)
```

```
2 of Diamonds
4 of Hearts
5 of Clubs
8 of Diamonds
```

To sort the cards, we can use the list method sort, which sorts the elements "in place" —that is, it modifies the list rather than creating a new list:

```
%%add_method_to Deck

    def sort(self):
        self.cards.sort()
```

When we invoke `sort`, it uses the `__lt__` method to compare cards:

```
deck.sort()
```

If we print the first few cards, we can confirm that they are in increasing order:

```
for card in deck.cards[:4]:
    print(card)
```

```
2 of Clubs
3 of Clubs
4 of Clubs
5 of Clubs
```

In this example, `Deck.sort` doesn't do anything other than invoke `list.sort`. Passing along responsibility like this is called **delegation**.

Parents and Children

Inheritance is the ability to define a new class that is a modified version of an existing class. As an example, let's say we want a class to represent a "hand," that is, the cards held by one player:

- A hand is similar to a deck—both are made up of a collection of cards, and both require operations like adding and removing cards.
- A hand is also different from a deck—there are operations we want for hands that don't make sense for a deck. For example, in poker we might compare two hands to see which one wins. In bridge, we might compute a score for a hand in order to make a bid.

This relationship between classes—where one is a specialized version of another—lends itself to inheritance.

To define a new class that is based on an existing class, we put the name of the existing class in parentheses:

```
class Hand(Deck):
    """Represents a hand of playing cards."""
```

This definition indicates that `Hand` inherits from `Deck`, which means that `Hand` objects can access methods defined in `Deck`, like `take_card` and `put_card`.

Hand also inherits `__init__` from `Deck`, but if we define `__init__` in the `Hand` class, it overrides the one in the `Deck` class:

```
%%add_method_to Hand

    def __init__(self, label=''):
        self.label = label
        self.cards = []
```

This version of `__init__` takes an optional string as a parameter, and always starts with an empty list of cards. When we create a `Hand`, Python invokes this method, not the one in `Deck`—which we can confirm by checking that the result has a `label` attribute:

```
hand = Hand('player 1')
hand.label
```

```
'player 1'
```

To deal a card, we can use `take_card` to remove a card from a `Deck`, and `put_card` to add the card to a `Hand`:

```
deck = Deck(cards)
card = deck.take_card()
hand.put_card(card)
print(hand)
```

```
Ace of Spades
```

Let's encapsulate this code in a `Deck` method called `move_cards`:

```
%%add_method_to Deck

    def move_cards(self, other, num):
        for i in range(num):
            card = self.take_card()
            other.put_card(card)
```

This method is polymorphic—that is, it works with more than one type: `self` and `other` can be either a `Hand` or a `Deck`. So we can use this method to deal a card from `Deck` to a `Hand`, from one `Hand` to another, or from a `Hand` back to a `Deck`.

When a new class inherits from an existing one, the existing one is called the **parent** and the new class is called the **child**. In general:

- Instances of the child class should have all of the attributes of the parent class, but they can have additional attributes.

- The child class should have all of the methods of the parent class, but it can have additional methods.
- If a child class overrides a method from the parent class, the new method should take the same parameters and return a compatible result.

This set of rules is called the "Liskov substitution principle" after computer scientist Barbara Liskov.

If you follow these rules, any function or method designed to work with an instance of a parent class, like a Deck, will also work with instances of a child class, like Hand. If you violate these rules, your code will collapse like a house of cards (sorry).

Specialization

Let's make a class called BridgeHand that represents a hand in bridge—a widely played card game. We'll inherit from Hand and add a new method called high_card_point_count that evaluates a hand using a "high card point" method, which adds up points for the high cards in the hand.

Here's a class definition that contains as a class variable a dictionary that maps from card names to their point values:

```
class BridgeHand(Hand):
    """Represents a bridge hand."""

    hcp_dict = {
        'Ace': 4,
        'King': 3,
        'Queen': 2,
        'Jack': 1,
    }
```

Given the rank of a card, like 12, we can use Card.rank_names to get the string representation of the rank, and then use hcp_dict to get its score:

```
rank = 12
rank_name = Card.rank_names[rank]
score = BridgeHand.hcp_dict.get(rank_name, 0)
rank_name, score
```

```
('Queen', 2)
```

The following method loops through the cards in a BridgeHand and adds up their scores:

```
%%add_method_to BridgeHand

    def high_card_point_count(self):
```

```
    count = 0
    for card in self.cards:
        rank_name = Card.rank_names[card.rank]
        count += BridgeHand.hcp_dict.get(rank_name, 0)
    return count
```

To test it, we'll deal a hand with five cards—a bridge hand usually has thirteen, but it's easier to test code with small examples:

```
hand = BridgeHand('player 2')

deck.shuffle()
deck.move_cards(hand, 5)
print(hand)
```

```
4 of Diamonds
King of Hearts
10 of Hearts
10 of Clubs
Queen of Diamonds
```

And here is the total score for the King and Queen:

```
hand.high_card_point_count()
```

```
5
```

BridgeHand inherits the variables and methods of Hand and adds a class variable and a method that are specific to bridge. This way of using inheritance is called **specialization** because it defines a new class that is specialized for a particular use, like playing bridge.

Debugging

Inheritance is a useful feature. Some programs that would be repetitive without inheritance can be written more concisely with it. Also, inheritance can facilitate code reuse, since you can customize the behavior of a parent class without having to modify it. In some cases, the inheritance structure reflects the natural structure of the problem, which makes the design easier to understand.

On the other hand, inheritance can make programs difficult to read. When a method is invoked, it is sometimes not clear where to find its definition—the relevant code may be spread across several modules.

Any time you are unsure about the flow of execution through your program, the simplest solution is to add print statements at the beginning of the relevant methods. If Deck.shuffle prints a message that says something like Running Deck.shuffle, then as the program runs it traces the flow of execution.

As an alternative, you could use the following function, which takes an object and a method name (as a string) and returns the class that provides the definition of the method:

```
def find_defining_class(obj, method_name):
    """
    """
    for typ in type(obj).mro():
        if method_name in vars(typ):
            return typ
    return f'Method {method_name} not found.'
```

find_defining_class uses the mro method to get the list of class objects (types) that will be searched for methods. "MRO" stands for "method resolution order," which is the sequence of classes Python searches to "resolve" a method name—that is, to find the function object the name refers to.

As an example, let's instantiate a BridgeHand and then find the defining class of shuffle:

```
hand = BridgeHand('player 3')
find_defining_class(hand, 'shuffle')
```

```
__main__.Deck
```

The shuffle method for the BridgeHand object is the one in Deck.

Glossary

inheritance: The ability to define a new class that is a modified version of a previously defined class.

encode: To represent one set of values using another set of values by constructing a mapping between them.

class variable: A variable defined inside a class definition, but not inside any method.

totally ordered: A set of objects is totally ordered if we can compare any two elements and the results are consistent.

delegation: When one method passes responsibility to another method to do most or all of the work.

parent class: A class that is inherited from.

child class: A class that inherits from another class.

specialization: A way of using inheritance to create a new class that is a specialized version of an existing class.

Exercises

Ask a Virtual Assistant

When it goes well, object-oriented programming can make programs more readable, testable, and reusable. But it can also make programs complicated and hard to maintain. As a result, OOP is a topic of controversy—some people love it, and some people don't.

To learn more about the topic, ask a virtual assistant:

- "What are some pros and cons of object-oriented programming?"
- "What does it mean when people say 'favor composition over inheritance'?"
- "What is the Liskov substitution principle?"
- "Is Python an object-oriented language?"
- "What are the requirements for a set to be totally ordered?"

And as always, consider using a virtual assistant to help with the following exercises.

Exercise

In contract bridge, a "trick" is a round of play in which each of four players plays one card. To represent those cards, we'll define a class that inherits from `Deck`:

```
class Trick(Deck):
    """Represents a trick in contract bridge."""
```

As an example, consider this trick, where the first player leads with the 3 of Diamonds, which means that Diamonds are the "led suit." The second and third players "follow suit," which means they play a card with the led suit. The fourth player plays a card of a different suit, which means they cannot win the trick. So the winner of this trick is the third player, because they played the highest card in the led suit:

```
cards = [Card(1, 3),
         Card(1, 10),
         Card(1, 12),
         Card(2, 13)]
trick = Trick(cards)
print(trick)
```

```
3 of Diamonds
10 of Diamonds
Queen of Diamonds
King of Hearts
```

Write a `Trick` method called `find_winner` that loops through the cards in the `Trick` and returns the index of the card that wins. In the previous example, the index of the winning card is 2.

Exercise

The next few exercises ask to you write functions that classify poker hands. If you are not familiar with poker, I'll explain what you need to know. We'll use the following class to represent poker hands:

```
class PokerHand(Hand):
    """Represents a poker hand."""

    def get_suit_counts(self):
        counter = {}
        for card in self.cards:
            key = card.suit
            counter[key] = counter.get(key, 0) + 1
        return counter

    def get_rank_counts(self):
        counter = {}
        for card in self.cards:
            key = card.rank
            counter[key] = counter.get(key, 0) + 1
        return counter
```

`PokerHand` provides two methods that will help with the exercises:

get_suit_counts
Loops through the cards in the `PokerHand`, counts the number of cards in each suit, and returns a dictionary that maps from each suit code to the number of times it appears.

get_rank_counts
Does the same thing with the ranks of the cards, returning a dictionary that maps from each rank code to the number of times it appears.

All of the exercises that follow can be done using only the Python features we have learned so far, but some of them are more difficult than most of the previous exercises. I encourage you to ask a virtual assistant for help.

For problems like this, it often works well to ask for general advice about strategies and algorithms. Then you can either write the code yourself or ask for code. If you ask for code, you might want to provide the relevant class definitions as part of the prompt.

As a first exercise, we'll write a method called `has_flush` that checks whether a hand has a "flush"—that is, whether it contains at least five cards of the same suit.

In most varieties of poker, a hand contains either five or seven cards, but there are some exotic variations where a hand contains other numbers of cards. But regardless of how many cards there are in a hand, the only ones that count are the five that make the best hand.

Exercise

Write a method called `has_straight` that checks whether a hand contains a straight, which is a set of five cards with consecutive ranks. For example, if a hand contains ranks 5, 6, 7, 8, and 9, it contains a straight.

An Ace can come before a 2 or after a King, so Ace, 2, 3, 4, 5 is a straight and so is 10, Jack, Queen, King, Ace. But a straight cannot "wrap around," so King, Ace, 2, 3, 4 is not a straight.

Exercise

A hand has a straight flush if it contains a set of five cards that are both a straight and a flush—that is, five cards of the same suit with consecutive ranks. Write a `PokerHand` method that checks whether a hand has a straight flush.

Exercise

A poker hand has a pair if it contains two or more cards with the same rank. Write a `PokerHand` method that checks whether a hand contains a pair.

You can use the following outline to get started.

To test your method, here's a hand that has a pair:

```
pair = deepcopy(bad_hand)
pair.put_card(Card(1, 2))
print(pair)
```

```
2 of Clubs
3 of Clubs
4 of Hearts
5 of Spades
7 of Clubs
2 of Diamonds
```

```
pair.has_pair()    # should return True
```

```
True
```

```
bad_hand.has_pair()     # should return False
```

```
False
```

```
good_hand.has_pair()    # should return False
```

```
False
```

Exercise

A hand has a full house if it contains three cards of one rank and two cards of another rank. Write a PokerHand method that checks whether a hand has a full house.

Exercise

This exercise is a cautionary tale about a common error that can be difficult to debug. Consider the following class definition:

```
class Kangaroo:
    """A Kangaroo is a marsupial."""

    def __init__(self, name, contents=[]):
        """Initialize the pouch contents.

        name: string
        contents: initial pouch contents.
        """
        self.name = name
        self.contents = contents

    def __str__(self):
        """Return a string representation of this Kangaroo.
        """
        t = [ self.name + ' has pouch contents:' ]
        for obj in self.contents:
            s = '    ' + object.__str__(obj)
            t.append(s)
        return '\n'.join(t)

    def put_in_pouch(self, item):
        """Adds a new item to the pouch contents.

        item: object to be added
        """
        self.contents.append(item)
```

__init__ takes two parameters: name is required, but contents is optional—if it's not provided, the default value is an empty list. __str__ returns a string representation of the object that includes the name and the contents of the pouch. put_in_pouch takes any object and appends it to contents.

Now let's see how this class works. We'll create two `Kangaroo` objects with the names Kanga and Roo:

```
kanga = Kangaroo('Kanga')
roo = Kangaroo('Roo')
```

To Kanga's pouch we'll add two strings and Roo:

```
kanga.put_in_pouch('wallet')
kanga.put_in_pouch('car keys')
kanga.put_in_pouch(roo)
```

If we print `kanga`, it seems like everything worked:

```
print(kanga)
```

```
Kanga has pouch contents:
    'wallet'
    'car keys'
    <__main__.Kangaroo object at 0x7f1f4f1a1330>
```

But what happens if we print `roo`?

```
print(roo)
```

```
Roo has pouch contents:
    'wallet'
    'car keys'
    <__main__.Kangaroo object at 0x7f1f4f1a1330>
```

Roo's pouch contains the same contents as Kanga's, including a reference to `roo`!

See if you can figure out what went wrong. Then ask a virtual assistant, "What's wrong with the following program?" and paste in the definition of `Kangaroo`.

CHAPTER 18

Python Extras

One of my goals for this book has been to teach you as little Python as possible. When there were two ways to do something, I picked one and avoided mentioning the other. Or sometimes I put the second one into an exercise.

Now I want to go back for some of the good bits that got left behind. Python provides a number of features that are not really necessary—you can write good code without them—but with them you can write code that's more concise, readable, or efficient, and sometimes all three.

Sets

Python provides a class called set that represents a collection of unique elements. To create an empty set, we can use the class object like a function:

```
s1 = set()
s1
```

```
set()
```

We can use the add method to add elements:

```
s1.add('a')
s1.add('b')
s1
```

```
{'a', 'b'}
```

Or we can pass any kind of sequence to set:

```
s2 = set('acd')
s2
```

```
{'a', 'c', 'd'}
```

An element can only appear once in a set. If you add an element that's already there, it has no effect:

```
s1.add('a')
s1
```

```
{'a', 'b'}
```

Or if you create a set with a sequence that contains duplicates, the result contains only unique elements:

```
set('banana')
```

```
{'a', 'b', 'n'}
```

Some of the exercises in this book can be done concisely and efficiently with sets. For example, here is a solution to an exercise in Chapter 11 that uses a dictionary to check whether there are any duplicate elements in a sequence:

```
def has_duplicates(t):
    d = {}
    for x in t:
        d[x] = True
    return len(d) < len(t)
```

This version adds the element of t as keys in a dictionary, and then checks whether there are fewer keys than elements. Using sets, we can write the same function like this:

```
def has_duplicates(t):
    s = set(t)
    return len(s) < len(t)
```

An element can only appear in a set once, so if an element in t appears more than once, the set will be smaller than t. If there are no duplicates, the set will be the same size as t.

set objects provide methods that perform set operations. For example, union computes the union of two sets, which is a new set that contains all elements that appear in either set:

```
s1.union(s2)
```

```
{'a', 'b', 'c', 'd'}
```

Some arithmetic operators work with sets. For example, the - operator performs set subtraction—the result is a new set that contains all elements from the first set that are *not* in the second set:

```
s1 - s2
```

```
{'b'}
```

In "Dictionary Subtraction" on page 177 we used dictionaries to find the words that appear in a document but not in a word list. We used the following function, which takes two dictionaries and returns a new dictionary that contains only the keys from the first that don't appear in the second:

```
def subtract(d1, d2):
    res = {}
    for key in d1:
        if key not in d2:
            res[key] = d1[key]
    return res
```

With sets, we don't have to write this function ourselves. If word_counter is a dictionary that contains the unique words in the document and word_list is a list of valid words, we can compute the set difference like this:

```
set(word_counter) - set(word_list)
```

The result is a set that contains the words in the document that don't appear in the word list.

The comparison operators work with sets. For example, <= checks whether one set is a subset of another, including the possibility that they are equal:

```
set('ab') <= set('abc')
```

```
True
```

With these operators, we can use sets to do some of the exercises in Chapter 7. For example, here's a version of uses_only that uses a loop:

```
def uses_only(word, available):
    for letter in word:
        if letter not in available:
            return False
    return True
```

uses_only checks whether all letters in word are in available. With sets, we can rewrite it like this:

```
def uses_only(word, available):
    return set(word) <= set(available)
```

If the letters in word are a subset of the letters in available, that means that word uses only the letters in available.

Counters

A Counter is like a set, except that if an element appears more than once, the Counter keeps track of how many times it appears. If you are familiar with the mathematical idea of a "multiset," a Counter is a natural way to represent a multiset.

The Counter class is defined in a standard module called collections, so you have to import it. Then you can use the class object as a function and pass as an argument a string, list, or any other kind of sequence:

```
from collections import Counter

counter = Counter('banana')
counter
```

```
Counter({'a': 3, 'n': 2, 'b': 1})
```

```
from collections import Counter

t = (1, 1, 1, 2, 2, 3)
counter = Counter(t)
counter
```

```
Counter({1: 3, 2: 2, 3: 1})
```

A Counter object is like a dictionary that maps from each key to the number of times it appears. As in dictionaries, the keys have to be hashable.

Unlike dictionaries, `Counter` objects don't raise an exception if you access an element that doesn't appear. Instead, they return `0`:

```
counter['d']
```

```
0
```

We can use `Counter` objects to solve one of the exercises from Chapter 10, which asks for a function that takes two words and checks whether they are anagrams—that is, whether the letters from one can be rearranged to spell the other.

Here's a solution using `Counter` objects:

```
def is_anagram(word1, word2):
    return Counter(word1) == Counter(word2)
```

If two words are anagrams, they contain the same letters with the same counts, so their `Counter` objects are equivalent.

`Counter` provides a method called `most_common` that returns a list of value-frequency pairs, sorted from most common to least:

```
counter.most_common()
```

```
[('a', 3), ('n', 2), ('b', 1)]
```

They also provide methods and operators to perform set-like operations, including addition, subtraction, union, and intersection. For example, the + operator combines two `Counter` objects and creates a new `Counter` that contains the keys from both and the sums of the counts.

We can test it by making a `Counter` with the letters from `'bans'` and adding it to the letters from `'banana'`:

```
counter2 = Counter('bans')
counter + counter2
```

```
Counter({'a': 4, 'n': 3, 'b': 2, 's': 1})
```

You'll have a chance to explore other `Counter` operations in the exercises at the end of this chapter.

defaultdict

The `collections` module also provides `defaultdict`, which is like a dictionary except that if you access a key that doesn't exist, it generates a new value automatically.

When you create a `defaultdict`, you provide a function that's used to create new values. A function that creates objects is sometimes called a **factory**. The built-in functions that create lists, sets, and other types can be used as factories.

For example, here's a `defaultdict` that creates a new `list` when needed:

```
from collections import defaultdict

d = defaultdict(list)
d
```

```
defaultdict(list, {})
```

Notice that the argument is `list`, which is a class object, not `list()`, which is a function call that creates a new list. The factory function doesn't get called unless we access a key that doesn't exist:

```
t = d['new key']
t
```

```
[]
```

The new list, which we're calling t, is also added to the dictionary. So if we modify t, the change appears in d:

```
t.append('new value')
d['new key']
```

```
['new value']
```

If you are making a dictionary of lists, you can often write simpler code using `defaultdict`.

In one of the exercises in Chapter 11, I made a dictionary that maps from a sorted string of letters to the list of words that can be spelled with those letters. For example, the string `'opst'` maps to the list `['opts', 'post', 'pots', 'spot', 'stop', 'tops']`.

Here's the original code:

```python
def all_anagrams(filename):
    d = {}
    for line in open(filename):
        word = line.strip().lower()
        t = signature(word)
        if t not in d:
            d[t] = [word]
        else:
            d[t].append(word)
    return d
```

And here's a simpler version using a `defaultdict`:

```python
def all_anagrams(filename):
    d = defaultdict(list)
    for line in open(filename):
        word = line.strip().lower()
        t = signature(word)
        d[t].append(word)
    return d
```

In the exercises at the end of the chapter, you'll have a chance to practice using `defaultdict` objects:

```python
from collections import defaultdict

d = defaultdict(list)
key = ('into', 'the')
d[key].append('woods')
d[key]
```

```
['woods']
```

Conditional Expressions

Conditional statements are often used to choose one of two values, like this:

```python
if x > 0:
    y = math.log(x)
else:
    y = float('nan')
```

This statement checks whether x is positive. If so, it computes its logarithm. If not, `math.log` would raise a `ValueError`. To avoid stopping the program, we generate a NaN, which is a special floating-point value that represents "Not a Number."

We can write this statement more concisely using a **conditional expression**:

```
y = math.log(x) if x > 0 else float('nan')
```

You can almost read this line like English: "y gets log-x if x is greater than 0; otherwise, it gets NaN."

Recursive functions can sometimes be written concisely using conditional expressions. For example, here is a version of `factorial` with a conditional *statement*:

```
def factorial(n):
    if n == 0:
        return 1
    else:
        return n * factorial(n-1)
```

And here's a version with a conditional *expression*:

```
def factorial(n):
    return 1 if n == 0 else n * factorial(n-1)
```

Another use of conditional expressions is handling optional arguments. For example, here is class definition with an __init__ method that uses a conditional statement to check a parameter with a default value:

```
class Kangaroo:
    def __init__(self, name, contents=None):
        self.name = name
        if contents is None:
            contents = []
        self.contents = contents
```

Here's a version that uses a conditional expression:

```
def __init__(self, name, contents=None):
    self.name = name
    self.contents = [] if contents is None else contents
```

In general, you can replace a conditional statement with a conditional expression if both branches contain a single expression and no statements.

List Comprehensions

In previous chapters, we've seen a few examples where we start with an empty list and add elements, one at a time, using the append method. For example, suppose we have a string that contains the title of a movie, and we want to capitalize all of the words:

```
title = 'monty python and the holy grail'
```

We can split it into a list of strings, loop through the strings, capitalize them, and append them to a list:

```
t = []
for word in title.split():
    t.append(word.capitalize())

' '.join(t)
```

```
'Monty Python And The Holy Grail'
```

We can do the same thing more concisely using a **list comprehension**:

```
t = [word.capitalize() for word in title.split()]

' '.join(t)
```

```
'Monty Python And The Holy Grail'
```

The bracket operators indicate that we are constructing a new list. The expression inside the brackets specifies the elements of the list, and the for clause indicates what sequence we are looping through.

The syntax of a list comprehension might seem strange, because the loop variable—word in this example—appears in the expression before we get to its definition. But you get used to it.

As another example, in "Making a Word List" on page 131 we used this loop to read words from a file and append them to a list:

```
word_list = []

for line in open('words.txt'):
    word = line.strip()
    word_list.append(word)
```

Here's how we can write that as a list comprehension:

```
word_list = [line.strip() for line in open('words.txt')]
```

A list comprehension can also have an `if` clause that determines which elements are included in the list. For example, here's a `for` loop we used in "Accumulating a List" on page 144 to make a list of only the words in `word_list` that are palindromes:

```
palindromes = []

for word in word_list:
    if is_palindrome(word):
        palindromes.append(word)
```

Here's how we can do the same thing with a list comprehension:

```
palindromes = [word for word in word_list if is_palindrome(word)]
```

When a list comprehension is used as an argument to a function, we can often omit the brackets. For example, suppose we want to add up $1/2^n$ for values of n from 0 to 9. We can use a list comprehension like this:

```
sum([1/2**n for n in range(10)])
```

```
1.998046875
```

Or we can leave out the brackets like this:

```
sum(1/2**n for n in range(10))
```

```
1.998046875
```

In this example, the argument is technically a **generator expression**, not a list comprehension, and it never actually makes a list. But other than that, the behavior is the same.

List comprehensions and generator expressions are concise and easy to read, at least for simple expressions. And they are usually faster than the equivalent `for` loops, sometimes much faster. So if you are mad at me for not mentioning them earlier, I understand.

But, in my defense, list comprehensions are harder to debug because you can't put a `print` statement inside the loop. I suggest you use them only if the computation is simple enough that you are likely to get it right the first time. Or consider writing and debugging a `for` loop and then converting it to a list comprehension.

any and all

Python provides a built-in function, any, that takes a sequence of boolean values and returns True if any of the values are True:

```
any([False, False, True])
```

```
True
```

any is often used with generator expressions:

```
any(letter == 't' for letter in 'monty')
```

```
True
```

That example isn't very useful because it does the same thing as the in operator. But we could use any to write concise solutions to some of the exercises in Chapter 7. For example, we can write uses_none like this:

```
def uses_none(word, forbidden):
    """Checks whether a word avoids forbidden letters."""
    return not any(letter in forbidden for letter in word)
```

This function loops through the letters in word and checks whether any of them are in forbidden. Using any with a generator expression is efficient because it stops immediately if it finds a True value, so it doesn't have to loop through the whole sequence.

Python provides another built-in function, all, that returns True if every element of the sequence is True. We can use it to write a concise version of uses_all:

```
def uses_all(word, required):
    """Check whether a word uses all required letters."""
    return all(letter in word for letter in required)
```

Expressions using any and all can be concise, efficient, and easy to read.

Named Tuples

The collections module provides a function called namedtuple that can be used to create simple classes. For example, the Point object in "Creating a Point" on page 233 has only two attributes, x and y.

Here's how we defined it:

```
class Point:
    """Represents a point in 2-D space."""

    def __init__(self, x, y):
        self.x = x
        self.y = y

    def __str__(self):
        return f'({self.x}, {self.y})'
```

That's a lot of code to convey a small amount of information. namedtuple provides a more concise way to define classes like this:

```
from collections import namedtuple

Point = namedtuple('Point', ['x', 'y'])
```

The first argument is the name of the class you want to create. The second is a list of the attributes Point objects should have. The result is a class object, which is why it is assigned to a capitalized variable name.

A class created with namedtuple provides an __init__ method that assigns values to the attributes and a __str__ that displays the object in a readable form. So we can create and display a Point object like this:

```
p = Point(1, 2)
p
```

```
Point(x=1, y=2)
```

Point also provides an __eq__ method that checks whether two Point objects are equivalent—that is, whether their attributes are the same:

```
p == Point(1, 2)
```

```
True
```

You can access the elements of a named tuple by name or by index:

```
p.x, p.y
```

```
(1, 2)
```

```
p[0], p[1]
```

```
(1, 2)
```

You can also treat a named tuple as a tuple, as in this assignment:

```
x, y = p
x, y
```

```
(1, 2)
```

But `namedtuple` objects are immutable. After the attributes are initialized, they can't be changed:

```
p[0] = 3
```

```
TypeError: 'Point' object does not support item assignment
```

```
p.x = 3
```

```
AttributeError: can't set attribute
```

`namedtuple` provides a quick way to define simple classes. The drawback is that simple classes don't always stay simple. You might decide later that you want to add methods to a named tuple. In that case, you can define a new class that inherits from the named tuple:

```
class Pointier(Point):
    """This class inherits from Point"""
```

Or at that point you could switch to a conventional class definition.

Packing Keyword Arguments

In "Argument Packing" on page 159, we wrote a function that packs its arguments into a tuple:

```
def mean(*args):
    return sum(args) / len(args)
```

You can call this function with any number of positional arguments:

```
mean(1, 2, 3)
```

```
2.0
```

But the * operator doesn't pack keyword arguments. So calling this function with a keyword argument causes an error:

```
mean(1, 2, start=3)
```

```
TypeError: mean() got an unexpected keyword argument 'start'
```

To pack keyword arguments, we can use the ** operator:

```
def mean(*args, **kwargs):
    print(kwargs)
    return sum(args) / len(args)
```

The keyword-packing parameter can have any name, but kwargs is a common choice. The result is a dictionary that maps from keywords to values:

```
mean(1, 2, start=3)
```

```
{'start': 3}
```

```
1.5
```

In this example, the value of kwargs is printed, but otherwise is has no effect.

But the ** operator can also be used in an argument list to unpack a dictionary. For example, here's a version of mean that packs any keyword arguments it gets and then unpacks them as keyword arguments for sum:

```
def mean(*args, **kwargs):
    return sum(args, **kwargs) / len(args)
```

Now if we call mean with start as a keyword argument, it gets passed along to sum, which uses it as the starting point of the summation. In the next example, start=3 adds 3 to the sum before computing the mean, so the sum is 6 and the result is 3:

```
mean(1, 2, start=3)
```

```
3.0
```

As another example, if we have a dictionary with keys x and y, we can use it with the unpack operator to create a Point object:

```
d = dict(x=1, y=2)
Point(**d)
```

```
Point(x=1, y=2)
```

Without the unpack operator, d is treated as a single positional argument, so it gets assigned to x, and we get a TypeError because there's no second argument to assign to y:

```
d = dict(x=1, y=2)
Point(d)
```

```
TypeError: Point.__new__() missing 1 required positional argument: 'y'
```

When you are working with functions that have a large number of keyword arguments, it is often useful to create and pass around dictionaries that specify frequently used options:

```
def pack_and_print(**kwargs):
    print(kwargs)

pack_and_print(a=1, b=2)
```

```
{'a': 1, 'b': 2}
```

Debugging

In previous chapters, we used doctest to test functions. For example, here's a function called add that takes two numbers and returns their sum. In includes a doctest that checks whether 2 + 2 is 4:

```
def add(a, b):
    '''Add two numbers.

    >>> add(2, 2)
    4
    '''
    return a + b
```

This function takes a function object and runs its doctests:

```
from doctest import run_docstring_examples

def run_doctests(func):
    run_docstring_examples(func, globals(), name=func.__name__)
```

So we can test add like this:

```
run_doctests(add)
```

There's no output, which means all tests passed.

Python provides another tool for running automated tests, called unittest. It is a little more complicated to use, but here's an example:

```
from unittest import TestCase

class TestExample(TestCase):

    def test_add(self):
        result = add(2, 2)
        self.assertEqual(result, 4)
```

First, we import TestCase, which is a class in the unittest module. To use it, we have to define a new class that inherits from TestCase and provides at least one test method. The name of the test method must begin with test and should indicate which function it tests.

In this example, test_add tests the add function by calling it, saving the result, and invoking assertEqual, which is inherited from TestCase. assertEqual takes two arguments and checks whether they are equal.

In order to run this test method, we have to run a function in unittest called main and provide several keyword arguments. The following function shows the details—if you are curious, ask a virtual assistant to explain how it works:

```
import unittest

def run_unittest():
    unittest.main(argv=[''], verbosity=0, exit=False)
```

run_unittest does not take TestExample as an argument—instead, it searches for classes that inherit from TestCase. Then it searches for methods that begin with test and runs them. This process is called **test discovery**.

Here's what happens when we call `run_unittest`:

```
run_unittest()
```

```
- - - - - - - - - - - - - - - - - - - - - - - - - - - - - - - - - - - - - - -
Ran 1 test in 0.000s

OK
```

`unittest.main` reports the number of tests it ran and the results. In this case OK indicates that the tests passed. To see what happens when a test fails, we'll add an incorrect test method to `TestExample`:

```
%%add_method_to TestExample

    def test_add_broken(self):
        result = add(2, 2)
        self.assertEqual(result, 100)
```

Here's what happens when we run the tests:

```
run_unittest()
```

```
======================================================================
FAIL: test_add_broken (__main__.TestExample)
- - - - - - - - - - - - - - - - - - - - - - - - - - - - - - - - - - - - - - -
Traceback (most recent call last):
  File "/tmp/ipykernel_29273/3833266738.py", line 3, in test_add_broken
    self.assertEqual(result, 100)
AssertionError: 4 != 100

- - - - - - - - - - - - - - - - - - - - - - - - - - - - - - - - - - - - - - -
Ran 2 tests in 0.000s

FAILED (failures=1)
```

The report includes the test method that failed and an error message showing where. The summary indicates that two tests ran and one failed.

In the following exercises, I'll suggest some prompts you can use to ask a virtual assistant for more information about `unittest`.

Glossary

factory: A function used to create objects, often passed as a parameter to a function.

conditional expression: An expression that uses a conditional to select one of two values.

list comprehension: A concise way to loop through a sequence and create a list.

generator expression: Similar to a list comprehension except that it does not create a list.

test discovery: A process used to find and run tests.

Exercises

Ask a Virtual Assistant

There are a few topics in this chapter you might want to learn about. Here are some questions to ask a virtual assistant:

- "What are the methods and operators of Python's set class?"
- "What are the methods and operators of Python's counter class?"
- "What is the difference between a Python list comprehension and a generator expression?"
- "When should I use Python's namedtuple rather than define a new class?"
- "What are some uses of packing and unpacking keyword arguments?"
- "How does unittest do test discovery?"
- "Along with assertequal, what are the most commonly used methods in unit test.TestCase?"
- "What are the pros and cons of doctest and unittest?"

For the following exercises, consider asking a virtual assistant for help, but as always, remember to test the results.

Exercise

One of the exercises in Chapter 7 asks for a function called uses_none that takes a word and a string of forbidden letters, and returns True if the word does not use any of the letters. Here's a solution:

```
def uses_none(word, forbidden):
    for letter in word.lower():
        if letter in forbidden.lower():
            return False
    return True
```

Write a version of this function that uses set operations instead of a for loop. Hint: ask a virtual assistant "How do I compute the intersection of Python sets?"

Exercise

Scrabble is a board game where the objective is to use letter tiles to spell words. For example, if we have tiles with the letters T, A, B, L, E, we can spell BELT and LATE using a subset of the tiles—but we can't spell BEET because we don't have two Es.

Write a function that takes a string of letters and a word, and checks whether the letters can spell the word, taking into account how many times each letter appears.

Exercise

In one of the exercises from Chapter 17, my solution to `has_straightflush` uses the following method, which partitions a `PokerHand` into a list of four hands, where each hand contains cards of the same suit:

```
def partition(self):
    """Make a list of four hands, each containing only one suit."""
    hands = []
    for i in range(4):
        hands.append(PokerHand())

    for card in self.cards:
        hands[card.suit].add_card(card)

    return hands
```

Write a simplified version of this function using a `defaultdict`.

Exercise

Here's the function from Chapter 11 that computes Fibonacci numbers:

```
def fibonacci(n):
    if n == 0:
        return 0

    if n == 1:
        return 1

    return fibonacci(n-1) + fibonacci(n-2)
```

Write a version of this function with a single `return` statement that uses two conditional expressions, one nested inside the other.

Exercise

The following is a function that recursively computes the binomial coefficient:

```
def binomial_coeff(n, k):
    """Compute the binomial coefficient "n choose k".

    n: number of trials
    k: number of successes

    returns: int
    """
    if k == 0:
        return 1

    if n == 0:
        return 0

    return binomial_coeff(n-1, k) + binomial_coeff(n-1, k-1)
```

Rewrite the body of the function using nested conditional expressions.

This function is not very efficient because it ends up computing the same values over and over. Make it more efficient by memoizing it, as described in "Memos" on page 146:

```
binomial_coeff(10, 4)    # should be 210
```

```
210
```

Exercise

Here's the __str__ method from the Deck class in "Printing the Deck" on page 256:

```
%%add_method_to Deck

    def __str__(self):
        res = []
        for card in self.cards:
            res.append(str(card))
        return '\n'.join(res)
```

Write a more concise version of this method with a list comprehension or generator expression.

CHAPTER 19

Final Thoughts

Learning to program is not easy, but if you made it this far, you are off to a good start. Now I have some suggestions for ways you can keep learning and apply what you have learned.

This book is meant to be a general introduction to programming, so we have not focused on specific applications. Depending on your interests, there are any number of areas where you can apply your new skills.

If you are interested in data science, there are three books of mine you might like:

- *Think Stats: Exploratory Data Analysis* (O'Reilly, 2014)
- *Think Bayes: Bayesian Statistics in Python* (O'Reilly, 2021)
- *Think DSP: Digital Signal Processing in Python* (O'Reilly, 2016)

If you are interested in physical modeling and complex systems, you might like:

- *Modeling and Simulation in Python: An Introduction for Scientists and Engineers* (No Starch Press, 2023)
- *Think Complexity: Complexity Science and Computational Modeling* (O'Reilly, 2018)

These use NumPy, SciPy, pandas, and other Python libraries for data science and scientific computing.

This book tries to find a balance between general principles of programming and details of Python. As a result, it does not include every feature of the Python language. For more about Python, and good advice about how to use it, I recommend *Fluent Python: Clear, Concise, and Effective Programming*, second edition by Luciano Ramalho (O'Reilly, 2022).

After an introduction to programming, a common next step is to learn about data structures and algorithms. I have a work in progress on this topic, called *Data Structures and Information Retrieval in Python*. A free electronic version is available from Green Tea Press (*https://greenteapress.com*).

As you work on more complex programs, you will encounter new challenges. You might find it helpful to review the sections in this book about debugging. In particular, remember the six Rs of debugging from "Debugging" on page 186: reading, running, ruminating, rubberducking, retreating, and resting.

This book suggests tools to help with debugging, including the `print` and `repr` functions, the `structshape` function in "Debugging" on page 166, and the built-in functions `isinstance`, `hasattr`, and `vars` in "Debugging" on page 219.

It also suggests tools for testing programs, including the `assert` statement, the `doctest` module, and the `unittest` module. Including tests in your programs is one of the best ways to prevent and detect errors, and save time debugging.

But the best kind of debugging is the kind you don't have to do. If you use an incremental development process, as described in "Incremental Development" on page 77, and test as you go, you will make fewer errors and find them more quickly when you do. Also, remember encapsulation and generalization from "Encapsulation and Generalization" on page 42, which is particularly useful when you are developing code in Jupyter notebooks.

Throughout this book, I've suggested ways to use virtual assistants to help you learn, program, and debug. I hope you are finding these tools useful.

In addition to virtual assistants like ChatGPT, you might also want to use a tool like Copilot that autocompletes code as you type. I did not recommend using these tools, initially, because they can be overwhelming for beginners. But you might want to explore them now.

Using AI tools effectively requires some experimentation and reflection to find a flow that works for you. If you think it's a nuisance to copy code from ChatGPT to Jupyter, you might prefer something like Copilot. But the cognitive work you do to compose a prompt and interpret the response can be as valuable as the code the tool generates, in the same vein as rubber duck debugging.

As you gain programming experience, you might want to explore other development environments. I think Jupyter notebooks are a good place to start, but they are relatively new and not as widely used as conventional integrated development environments (IDEs). For Python, the most popular IDEs include PyCharm and Spyder—and Thonny, which is often recommended for beginners. Other IDEs, like Visual Studio Code and Eclipse, work with other programming languages as well. Or, as a simpler alternative, you can write Python programs using any text editor you like.

As you continue your programming journey, you don't have to go alone! If you live in or near a city, there's a good chance there is a Python user group you can join. These groups are usually friendly to beginners, so don't be afraid. If there is no group near you, you might be able to join events remotely. Also, keep an eye out for regional Python conferences.

One of the best ways to improve your programming skills is to learn another language. If you are interested in statistics and data science, you might want to learn R. But I particularly recommend learning a functional language like Racket or Elixir. Functional programming requires a different kind of thinking, which changes the way you think about programs.

Good luck!

Index

About the Author

Allen Downey is a staff producer at Brilliant and professor emeritus at Olin College of Engineering. He has taught computer science at Wellesley College, Colby College, and UC Berkeley. He has a Ph.D. in computer science from UC Berkeley and a master's degree from MIT.

Colophon

The animal on the cover of *Think Python* is a plum-headed parakeet (*Psittacula cyanocephala*), a vibrant bird native to the Indian subcontinent.

This medium-sized parrot is known for the male's dazzling plum-colored head, while females have a grayish-blue head, with both sexes with different shades of green on their chest, belly, wings, and back. Their long tails are a cool bluish-green tipped with white, adding a touch of elegance. As seen in the cover image, males have a black chin stripe and a narrow black band around their neck, bordered by a vibrant turquoise, with a distinctive red shoulder patch. Females lack these markings and often have a yellow collar instead.

These social birds flit through well-wooded areas in large flocks, their flight patterns a flurry of twists and turns accompanied by high-pitched calls. They are also acrobatic climbers, adept at navigating branches and using their strong beaks to explore nooks and crannies for food; their diet consists mainly of fruits, seeds, and blossoms.

The plum-headed parakeet's population is considered Least Concern by the IUCN but with a decreasing trend, highlighting the need for conservation efforts. Many of the animals on O'Reilly covers are endangered; all of them are important to the world.

The color illustration is by Karen Montgomery, based on an antique line engraving from a loose plate, source unknown. The series design is by Edie Freedman, Ellie Volckhausen, and Karen Montgomery. The cover fonts are Gilroy Semibold and Guardian Sans. The text font is Adobe Minion Pro; the heading font is Adobe Myriad Condensed; and the code font is Dalton Maag's Ubuntu Mono.

Milton Keynes UK
Ingram Content Group UK Ltd.
UKHW051538210924
448609UK00002B/12